SHAFTESBURY

G. F. A. Best

Geoffrey Best was born in 1928 and educated at St Paul's School, Trinity College, Cambridge and Harvard. He has lectured at many universities, including Cambridge, Edinburgh (where he was Sir Richard Lodge Professor of History), Chicago, York (Toronto) and Oxford. He was the co-editor of VICTORIAN STUDIES 1958–70 and in July 1974 was elected to the Council of Victorian Society. Since 1974 he has been Professor of History at the University of Sussex.

Shaftesbury

G. F. A. Best

NEW ENGLISH LIBRARY
TIMES MIRROR

First published by B. T. Batsford Ltd., 1964
Copyright © by G. F. A. Best 1964

*

FIRST NEL MENTOR EDITION 1975

*

NEL Mentor Books are published by The New English Library Limited from
Barnard's Inn, Holborn, London E.C.1. Made and printed in Great Britain by
C. Nicholls & Company Ltd.

450022579

PREFACE

WHATEVER the faults of this book, I alone am responsible for them. Whatever merits it may be thought to possess, are partly due to other people; principal among whom is Admiral of the Fleet the Earl Mountbatten, to whom I am deeply indebted for permission to use Lord Shaftesbury's manuscript diaries, from the Broadlands archives. No significant use has been made of these, I believe, since the great man's first and best biographer, his friend Edwin Hodder, incorporated copious transcriptions from them in the three-volume *Life and Works of the seventh Earl of Shaftesbury* he published in 1886. Hodder's selection was actually very fair and representative as well as copious and, for its day, unusually frank. But of course there was a good deal of the diary he thought fit to leave out or merely to hint at: uncomplimentary references to persons like Queen Victoria, whose feelings he did not wish or dare to hurt; the nastiest remarks about persons like Mr Gladstone whom he did not much mind hurting; the most private or peculiar of his subject's reflections on religious, political and family matters, and so on.

My brief biography in no sense replaces Hodder, who must always be the first recourse for those with time to read a classic Victorian biography. I venture to hope, however, that even students of Hodder may find this book useful as a supplement and, sometimes, a corrective. I also hope that I have not failed duly to deal with the most important aspects of Shaftesbury's long life and many works, giving as fair an account of them as can be given in fifty-five thousand words. Such an account, of such a man, has proved quite incompatible with a simple chronological treatment. It has been necessary to fasten tenaciously on to the situations, ideas and activities that showed him most vividly as he really was, or constituted his main claims to be regarded as a great man and, in a way that would seem to be rivalled by few other individual great Britons, a shaper of modern Britain. Where the course of time does reveal definite change in his character or ideas, I have of course noticed it in the appropriate place.

My first debt of gratidue is due, then, to the owner of the diaries upon which much of what is new in this book is based. But I am very grateful also to Miss D. M. Coates and her colleagues at the National Register of Archives for the patient and good-humoured assistance that only those who have experienced it can properly appreciate; to Mr George Howard for allowing me to examine and use the papers of the seventh Earl of Carlisle, at Castle Howard; to Prof Philip Collins for much valuable information; to the Reverend Dr John Kent for helpful comments on chapter three; to Professor Norman Gash for identifying the characters in 'Jack Cade's Insurrection'; and finally to my wife who, besides correcting the English and compiling the index, put up with a great deal before those stages were reached.

ACKNOWLEDGMENT

The Author and Publishers wish to thank The Mansell Collection for permission to reproduce the line illustrations on pages 41 and 145.

CONTENTS

Line Illustrations in the text

I

CHILDHOOD, MARRIAGE
AND FAMILY

FROM nothing in Ashley's ancestry, parentage or upbringing could anyone possibly have foreseen that he would develop the way he did. He was moreover a long time developing. Born on 28 April 1801, it was 1828 before he took up – almost accidentally, as it would seem – his first characteristic good work, and 1833 before – again by accident – he took up the one that first made him famous. His marriage, in 1830, was of momentous importance to him. Some time soon thereafter he became, as he was to remain for the rest of his days, an ardent Evangelical. The Ashley we know only comes into clear focus in his early thirties.

He was nothing like any of the Ashleys that had gone before. The first of them, Anthony Ashley Cooper, Baron Ashley of Wimborne St Giles's from 1661, created Earl of Shaftesbury in 1672, is best known as Dryden's Achitophel, the near-satanic portrait of a Whig politician. The second was a nullity, and mentally subnormal. The third was an amiable, deistical *littérateur* and philosopher, one of the founders of the 'moral sense' school, whose well-mannered works achieved celebrity under their collective title, *Characteristics of Men, Manners, Opinions and Times*. Neither the fourth nor the fifth made any mark.

The sixth Earl, Cropley Ashley Cooper, the fifth's younger brother, had, however, one claim to distinction in his own right, besides being our Ashley's father. Soon after his arrival in the House of Lords, in 1811, he took over the chairmanship of committees during the regular chairman's illness; he was so good at it, that the peers made him their permanent chairman in 1814; and he held the post (for which he was paid £1,500 a year) until the beginning of 1851, when his resignation preceded his death by only a few months. For no other work is he commemorated. He represented the borough of Dorchester from 1790 until 1811, but history does not record what else he did during the twenty-one years between his coming of age and his succession to the title. The presumption must be, that he did nothing out of the ordinary. The *Annual Register*'s obituary notice described him as 'a man of undignified presence, of indistinct and hurried speech, of hasty and brusque manner'. His treatment of his children was callous and peremptory. None of them loved him – although they loved their mother, a daughter of the fourth Duke of Marlborough, even less. A few days after his father's death, Ashley, trying commendably hard to feel filial and charitable, noted that 'his besetting defect was self-satisfaction and self-confidence; he could not believe that a word, or an action or a thought, or a habit – anything he did, nor anything that he omitted, could be wrong'. But the very qualities that made him an odious parent and a generally repulsive person helped to make him an excellent chairman, linked as they evidently were in his case to a good head for business, a terse and prompt utterance, scrupulous integrity and judicial impartiality and a devotion to the public service. His post in the House of Lords was no sinecure, nor were its rigours compensated by the glamour of popularity. Although his role in getting the business of the upper house done can hardly have been much less significant than the Lord Chancellor's, it was much less publicized, and only his peers and the most knowledgeable of the political public were equipped to appreciate it. He was not the least worthy of the public servants of his day, performing efficiently and without ostentation an important job which not every peer would have liked, and few perhaps have done so well. He seems to have done it, moreover, as much from a sense of duty as from any other motive. That said, there is no more to be said in his favour. The biographer of his eldest son and heir must go on to say something against.

Ashley's parents held in an extreme form an attitude towards their children by no means uncommon among the British aristocracy. Comradeship between parents and children, the active participation by parents – especially the mothers – in

the education of their offspring, the acceptance of children as
having a legitimate and for the parents even a rewarding claim
on their parents' time and attention, and in brief everything
comprised under the title of 'family life', are actually very
recent phenomena in the history of humanity. In Britain the
idea of family life probably began among the middling classes
of society during the sixteenth and seventeenth centuries;
from there it subsequently infiltrated upwards and downwards.
Just how far it had got amongst the aristocracy by the
beginning of the nineteenth century would be difficult to
reckon; but certainly it had not yet got anywhere near the
Shaftesburys.

Ashley grew up without any experience of parental love.
He saw little of his parents, and when duty or necessity compelled them to take notice of him they were formal and
frightening. They left their children to be looked after by
servants and schoolteachers, and were satisfied so long as the
children were presentable for inspection when required. They
worked on the convenient principle, sanctioned by most of the
theologians of the day, that it was positively for a child's good
to learn, through fear of its parents, the proper orthodox fear
of God; finding it also very much to their convenience, as the
same theologians might have realized had they been intelligent
enough, to dispense wholly with the less fearful attributes of
the divine sovereignty. To the hardships and unhappiness of
their children, they remained indifferent, and they were spared
any embarrassing direct awareness of them by the children's
inability to mention the subject. So, whether at Rosedale
House in Richmond, their summer residence until 1811, or at
24 Grosvenor Square, where they spent the winter, little Lord
Ashley had a wretched time of it, 'left, with his sisters (all of
whom were older than himself), to the tender mercies of the
servants . . . he knew, times without number, what it was to be
kept for days without sufficient food until he was pinched
with starvation; and could recall many weary nights in winter
when he lay awake all through the long hours, suffering from
cold'.[1]

1 Hodder, i. 41–2.

School might, under such circumstances, have offered an escape into a brighter world; but the school to which Ashley was sent from 1808 to 1813, Manor House, in Chiswick Lane, offered merely an alternative and more disgusting range of horrors. In later life Shaftesbury, when he could bring himself to mention it at all, never did so but with a shudder. 'I think there never was such a wicked school before or since,' he once wrote. 'The place was bad, wicked, filthy; and the treatment was starvation and cruelty.' Again: 'Nothing could have surpassed it for filth, bullying, neglect, and hard treatment of every sort. . . . It was very similar to Dotheboys Hall.' Yet Manor House, six miles or so to the west of Hyde Park Corner, catered expensively for the sons of gentry and professional people, not cheaply, in a remote and inhospitable corner of Yorkshire, for orphans, bastards, and the unwanted offspring of first marriages; and its proprietor was no Wackford Squeers but a respectable doctor of divinity, Thomas Horne, formerly fellow of Trinity College, Oxford, one of whose sons would soon be Attorney-General. This was the unfeeling, unconscientious side of the English *ancien régime* of which Ashley was to become a principal reformer. His first and worst school apparently left him (as such schools did not always leave their victims) unscarred in body; but how deeply scarred in mind, we can only guess. He seems to have gone no further than supposing that 'it may have given me an early horror of oppression and cruelty'. He hardly needed Dr Horne's treatment to give him first-hand experience of that. Parents, home and school must together have contributed to form that melancholic air, that tense and rigid self-possession, that hypersensitive heart and that secret longing for love and admiration which marked him for the rest of his life.

Some small shelter from the misery and desolation of his first twelve years he got from two sources of limited and occasional value; from the housekeeper, and from his sisters. From Maria Millis, alone of the servants who had such complete charge over him, he received affection; and he received also, what he subsequently always considered even more important, his first ideas of religion. No doubt he was dragooned to church on Sundays, and made to go through certain disciplined devotional motions at school; but none of this, of course, could touch him. What did touch him was the reality, and the homely practicality, of the love which her Christianity made her feel towards the unhappy child. She told him Bible stories, she taught him a prayer; and when she died, just after he had gone to Manor House, she left him her watch, which he wore to the end of his life. Other and more sophisticated religious influences must have come to bear upon him between leaving Manor House and his conversion to full-blown Evangelicalism about twenty years later, but none can have shaped his early mind so much. Of his sisters and younger brothers during their early years we can discover nothing; but it is not rash to surmise that he early came to feel that watchful and jealous affection for them which he continued to show, so far as they or their spouses would let him, when they were grown up and married. This affection led him to what were probably his first exercises in philanthropy, when as a young man he ventured to shield them, so far as his dependent circumstances permitted, against the cruelty of their parents, and to create for them more happy and hopeful a life. 'Good heavens,' he wrote on 24 December 1828, 'how I wish that Harriet were married! Her life is heavy and without solace; what will it be hereafter? She has refused many, but I cannot blame her, for they were not men of a quality to become her fit companions. . . . The whole range of womankind could not furnish a wife so perfect as she would be. . . .' She did find a husband, of whom he approved, in 1830. Charlotte, who married in 1824, was an especial object of the father's cruelty. 'Having for years vented malignity and horror against Charlotte, he has ceased only because his children have answered him *sternly*' (16 November 1829). But to answer such a father sternly must have taken a lot of doing, and of course it only made his relations with his parents worse. He tried to keep out of his mother's way as much as he could. Her hardness was unbearable. 'Away with her memory! The idea of such fiend-warmed hearts is bad for a christian soul' (28 April 1826). When he later found himself suspecting a very sweet girl

because of her mother's dubious reputation, he checked himself thus: 'Have I not seen daughters the very reverse of their
mothers, domestic, loving, faithful? If the world were to judge
of *my own sister* by the infernal wickedness of the parent that
bore us, would the conclusion be true? (2 August 1829).

As for the parent that begat them, Ashley's dutiful endeavours to please and propitiate him were fruitless, and one
may well suppose that, had Ashley not, as the eldest son, been
inextricably tied to the succession to the title and the estate,
the father would have cut him off completely. As it was,
however, neither could be completely independent of the other.
Ashley's consent was, for example, indispensable in some
transactions relating to the family estates; and once at least he
lent his father money.

Not a year has passed in which I have not conferred some favour
on him [he noted on 16 November 1829] and not a year has passed
in which I have not received an insult open or implied. His very
civilities are a constraint to him; his natural tendency is to avoid
me and all his children; he has refused them a home. . . . *He com-
manded* me to leave his house in London, and will receive me
nowhere else – is this right? During four years, with the exception
of one week passed in Dorsetshire, I have not broken bread in his
house ten times. . . . As to friendship and affection between him and
me, years of experience have sufficiently proved that outward
civility and *only* civility is the utmost that can be looked for, and
this by no means of certain calculation unless we should be infre-
quent and short in our interviews.

They kept out of each other's way as much as they could.

Being thus destitute of family, home and of parental
affection, Ashley sought them elsewhere; and the record of
his life between his coming of age and his marriage is mainly
one of a search for love and support, while living the normal
life of a respectable young aristocrat about town, distinguished
from his contemporaries mainly by his withdrawals into
introspection, alternatively moody and rapturous, and by the
gravity and religious earnestness – it was not yet Evangelical
zeal – which governed alike his social conduct and his first
essays in philanthropy.

The thirteen years that lay between his leaving Manor House and his formal entry into public life, as Tory member for Woodstock, may be quickly dealt with. They always seemed to him to have been largely wasted, and they clearly played no important part in his development. From Manor House he went for a couple of years to Harrow, which he quite enjoyed. The next two years he spent in the home of a clerical relative in Derbyshire. 'I was sent there', he subsequently wrote, 'to be got out of the way, for the clergyman never professed that he was able to teach me anything, nor, indeed did my father require of him any such services. . . . I hardly ever opened a book, and seldom heard anything that was worth hearing; nevertheless there were constantly floating in my mind all sorts of aspirations, though I never took a step to make their fulfilment possible.' His father then allowed himself to be persuaded by some older friend of Ashley's (possibly the third Earl Bathurst, who, with his gentle and pious wife, was very kind to Ashley during the twenties) to send him not into the army but to Oxford. He went up to Christ Church in 1819, recovered habits of application so successfully that he got a First, and began a wide-ranging course of reading – everything from the novel of the hour to astronomy and theology – that came to give some depth and substance to those 'aspirations' of his. They bubbled up all the time: 'Visions without end,' he recorded on his twenty-fifth birthday, 'but, God be praised, all of a noble character. I fancy myself in wealth and power, exerting my influence for the ends that I sought it for, for the increase of religion and true happiness. I conceive myself the best, the wisest, the most zealous of Ministers; the best, the warmest, the ablest of friends. . . .' At the same time he was examining his character with a keen edge of ruthless and dispassionate self-awareness that partisan Evangelicalism was later to blunt.

During the last three years I have cured myself of several defects. They were almost vices, perhaps quite so. I am the happier for it. I wish that a keen sensibility to anything like coldness or temporary indifference from my friends were subdued. It leads me to frequent mistakes by the unreflecting quickness of my feelings. . . . I wish too that the few sparks of love of distinction were for ever smothered. The embers are kept under but now and then some fuel incautiously dropped excites a flame.

From these acute self-questionings he lapsed directly into the more commonplace language of self-depreciation which compensated his thirst for fame and success till the end of his days: '. . . it is enough that I am neither gifted, learned, nor profitable; after all I am only numbered with the crowd; let me endeavour then to do my duty in this state of insignificance; and in another world, God helping.'

He entered the House of Commons in the autumn of 1826, and at once entered upon the normal course of political apprenticeship, which promised ministerial office very soon to an aristocrat of such abilities. His guiding principles, both orthodox Tory ones, were an eager Protestantism and a proud determination to keep Great Britain supreme (as he unquestioningly assumed it was, in religion and civic virtue as well as in empire and commerce) among the nations. The Duke of Wellington quickly became his patron and hero. Canning seems at first to have divided with the Duke Ashley's rather adolescent hero worship. Although lamentably lax in his views on the 'Catholic Question', he expressed a view of Britain's international power and beneficence which Ashley applauded in language of stiring warmth; but the political crisis which filled the early spring of 1827 soon blew up, to teach Ashley his first hard lesson in politics: namely, that if one was going to work in with the existing parties (and there was no other way to office), it was no good judging men exclusively by one's own standards and affections. Lord Liverpool had a stroke, and retired; 'Dukey', as Ashley was now naming him, and Peel, the only Tory commoner with anything like Canning's ability, declined to co-operate with Canning in forming a new administration; and Ashley took their side, being persuaded to reverse his own views of Canning and uncritically to swallow theirs, which had become viciously partisan. Needing a political director less Olympian than the Duke, he nestled into Peel's cool shadow, where he was to remain for the next fifteen years:

May 20th, Sunday. – Dined yesterday and met Peel. . . . Read Canning's letter to the D. of W.; a mixture of apology and accusation, alternately fierceness and truckling, which do no honour to his principles. God bless Dukey, what a noble answer! I am now convinced that blackest treachery [the next few words are illegible] . . . frightful falsehood to his king and country, and am I to trust this man? God protect me from it! I like Peel. I love honesty and truth. He is become friendly also. I hear that he and Dukey speak most highly of me. I shall never want more than the praises of true gentlemen. . . .

This incident, of no great importance in itself, is interesting as an illumination of several permanent aspects of Ashley's complicated character. He was in many ways unstable. He was quick to make extreme judgments, and as quick, sometimes, to unmake them; but then he was quite likely to go and make the same (wrong) judgment again! Sometimes perceptively self-critical, and successful in some departments of self-control, he rarely saw this defect in himself, and never corrected it.[1] From it came the harsh snap-judgments and repetitious moralizings that filled his diary year after years. Yet his very instability saved him from some of the undesirable consequences which this habit of mind invited. Diffident and self-critical as well as ambitious and vain, as quick to admire and applaud as to suspect and distrust, his affections and enthusiasms were often inconstant; and so the traits which could make him (at least in his secret thoughts) an unreliable friend could also work to save him from the flatterers and toadies to whom he was a natural prey. Peel was flattering Ashley in the spring of 1827. Canning and Peel, as the breach between them opened, each set out to catch this promising new recruit. Peel and 'Dukey' won. Within a matter of days – hours, almost – Ashley was faithfully echoing their expressions of violent detestation of Canning. When Canning died, three months later, Ashley softened his tone sufficiently

1 One such rare occasion was, for instance, when he was highly worked up about the Jerusalem Bishopric Bill. On 17 September 1841 he denounced Sir Robert Inglis, 'the lover of forms', for obstructing it; five days later he had changed his tune to 'Inglis has behaved admirably; he is a good man, and I, an excitable one!'

to 'lament his fate in charity', but if he ever felt any twinge
of regret at having swung so extravagantly from one side to
the other, or any awareness that he was silly to have done so,
no sign of it appears in his diary. His inconstancy in this
instance could be attributed to immaturity and inexperience,
were it not to continue fitfully for the rest of his life. Peel
himself was later to become a principal sufferer by it, as
Ashley's mind rushed from praise and belief to censure and
suspicion. His starry-eyed reverence for the Duke (for example
on 3 May 1827 he said; 'Whatever is open, manly and noble
in simplicity, shone forth in his speech. Truth and honour
were never more conspicuous, and while the great hero was'
defending himself in the full assembly of the British peers,
a halo of glory and merit seemed to enwrap his whole form and
visage') received in 1831 the first of a series of disillusionings
which a more balanced and cautious mind would never have
invited.[1] Indeed, most of the statesmen with whom he had
dealings went through the same mill; and it is perhaps
significant that the only great one who never set his teeth on
edge was Palmerston. There were several excellent reasons
for this, as we shall in due course see; but to them might well
have been added some recognition – subconscious perhaps –
that here was a supreme example of the balanced and infinitely
good-natured mind, extravagant neither in praise nor blame,
an exemplar of several qualities that Ashley lacked.

Early in 1828 the Duke made him a junior minister for the
Board of Control (i.e. the India Office). He seems to have
carried out his duties efficiently. In 1829 he followed his
leaders into voting for the concession of political equality to
Roman Catholics – a volte-face he later came to regret.
Eighteen months later he followed them out of office. Palmerston, newly appointed Foreign Secretary of Earl Grey's
administration, offered him his Under-Secretaryship. Ashley
refused; he wished no one to doubt his Toryism. In the general
election which preceded that change of government he became
member for Dorchester. The following year, 1831, the
intensity of his dislike for Grey's parliamentary reforms

1 See Hodder, i. 118–23.

propelled him to contest the more important constituency of the county of Dorset; he was elected, and he continued to represent it until another volte-face, over the corn laws, induced him to resign at the end of January 1846. Meanwhile he remained faithful to Sir Robert Peel. In December 1834, when Peel undertook with many misgivings to form a minority government, he offered Ashley a junior office at the Admiralty, which Ashley with much reluctance accepted. He felt he should have been offered something better. From about this time appears to date the growing distrust and dislike of Peel which contributed to keep Ashley out of Peel's administration in 1841. As time went by, Ashley ceased to be the good party man he had begun as, and became a sort of free-lance Tory; as he became increasingly identified with the various topics of social reform he had made his own, this semi-detached parliamentary position came to be recognized as appropriate; and it is perhaps to Peel's credit that he never responded to Ashley's free-lance activities (which were politically sometimes embarrassing) by any denial of his essential Toryism. Unpredictable and singular though Ashley was for most of his life, Liberal though his favourite son was to become, the Toryism of his years of political apprenticeship stuck.

Through those earliest years, however, neither politics nor religion nor philanthropy were his main concern. What seems principally to have bothered him was his desire to get married. His diaries only start properly in 1826, so we cannot be sure how much it was bothering him before then. But it was clearly his main emotional concern between 1826 and 1830 when at last he managed it.

He learnt the nature and power of love while visiting Vienna during, or just before, the winter of 1825–6. He fell in love there with a certain Antoinette. The excision of many pages, the deletion of some sentences from his first diary, prevent us from knowing much about her. He was passionately attracted to her at the time, and for the rest of his life was apt to recall, with no self-reproach and little regret, in the tranquillity of his subsequent happy marriage, the exalting emotions of his days with her. Enough was left in the first of the diaries, and enough admitted (with, as one would expect, diminishing frequency) in the later ones, to prove that, hard though he was in some ways, anything connected with love, marriage and children always brought out his tenderest side. But this first attachment seems to have been an impossible one. Antoinette was lovely and desirable – 'she was, and is, an angel', he recorded, on 28 May 1826, soon after he was home again; 'but she was surrounded by, and would have brought with her, a halo of hell. I thought the Deity harsh in the obstacles to our union, obstacles which he raised in my own mind even; but now I confess his wisdom and tender providence. . . .' Was she a Roman Catholic? Had she no fortune at all? Were her relations disreputable? It must have been some barrier of this order that stood in the way.

But he still thought of her affectionately. On 13 August 1827, for instance: 'A man loves fiercely but once; the next time is reason or convenience, or fancy, or plain matter of fact.' Then, apostrophizing her:

You are now married, and happy as one so thwarted and repressed can be with the aid of talent and religion. Two years have gone by; she has been oftentimes out of my memory, not through the presence of another but lost in new business and active life. Solitude however brings her back, and though I remember all with sorrow, there is now much to soothe, nay even to delight in. . . .

A friend tried to cure him by pointing out her imperfections. Lord Clanwilliam, who must have been in Vienna with him and stayed on after he had left, reported unfavourably on her subsequent behaviour, and Ashley, characteristically, was for the moment swayed.

Clanwilliam talks of her Italian blood, her amours with Fritz [Somebody], her wanton liberties, her everything short of positive crimes. – Why, good God, I had thought her [illegible] . . . and ignorant even of natural sensation. . . . A year ago I should have murdered the man who talked thus, but I am now less eager and can listen. . . . Surely the mother and daughter must consider me as the very silliest puppy they ever associated with.

But this conversion was only temporary, and skin deep. On 29 January 1829 Princess Esterhazy told him how Antoinette had died a few days after childbirth. 'Liebe, Liebe herself is dead,' he exclaimed. He carefully recalled all his hours with her, took out from some secret place a scarf of hers and mourned over it, thought of 'the many walks, the many sentiments, the many tears we have known together. . . .' He never wholly forgot them.

But these affectionate and mournful reveries were not allowed to interrupt the main business of his life, the finding of a wife better adapted than Antoinette could have been to life among the English aristocracy. On 2 August 1829, for instance, even while he was reading Jortin's *Evidences* – 'Again the thoughts of marriage come over me; on this head I am most prudential in my conclusions; God alone knows how I shall be in my choice . . I am now 28, and it suits neither with my dignity nor my principles to continue the life of a headstrong youngster just emancipated from college. . . .' It would mean a narrowing of the bounds of life and, of course, financial difficulties, 'but there are joys and honours and respectabilities and means of excellence in marriage' and, moreover, ' "it is better to marry than to burn" . . . .'

Poor Lord Ashley! Affectionate, passionate, impressionable, and for all his sobriety far from unsociable, his was a painful path through all those dinners, dances and parties of the *beau monde* to which he had been born and bred, trying to find that wife who alone, he knew in his heart, could bring him to life, free him from the parental terrors that still beset him, and make him useful in the world. For so many others, it was so much easier. Many of his contemporaries had more money or fewer scruples; some only wanted wives as mistresses, brood-mares or slaves; companionship figured less, often hardly at all, in their ideas of marriage; they could leave so much more to the decisions of their parents, or the drifts of convention. But Ashley had a father whom he unsuccessfully tried to like, a mother whom he unsuccessfully tried to think he did not hate, a yearning for a family life he had only glimpsed through barred doors, a high-principled dislike of convention, an unusually exacting taste for both looks and intelligence.

In solitude very often of late I somehow begin to feel how truly God pronounced, 'It is not good for man to be alone', but still I had rather be alone than have a wife inferior to the imaginary darling whom I have adored for nearly a whole year. . . . Methinks that if I could find the creature I have invented, I should love her with a tenderness and truth unprecedented in the history of wedlock. . . . [24 September 1828.]

No wonder he found it as difficult as desirable to escape from the lonely dangers of bachelor life! No wonder he stood rather at the edge of the party, handsome, grave, enigmatic, looking always for the glance that might suggest some inner grace, listening for the variation in the small-talk that might reveal some unexpected individuality, praying for God's help in his great and urgent quest.

The spring of 1829 was preoccupied with an attempt to marry the third Earl of Liverpool's seventeen-year-old daughter, Lady Selina Jenkinson, whom (unless this was yet another girl) he first noticed at the opera. 'Shall I or shall I not proceed to make further investigation? I pray heaven to counsel me . . .' (22 March 1829). Her cousin, Lady C. Cavendish, to whom on 29 April 1829 he opened his case, was not encouraging. Her family would not consider him 'as offering advantages at all similar to those she would bring'. But he persisted, found her 'captivating', and on 6 May 1829 even pursued her to a ball – 'Oh what a place for nurturing a love such as I wish to feel!' Within a month, however, it was all over. Her father decisively and apparently insultingly warned him off. By 2 July 1829 it was:

I shall not think of you any more, Madame Selina. . . . How odd that I should ever have fancied you! You are stiff as a poker, with no more grace in your movements than a pair of tongs, but see the effect of imagination. . . . Perhaps these, many might remark, are sour grapes; it may be, but sweet or sour, we shall never eat them together; so I wish you well, and myself a little more discernment and patience in my next inquiry after domestic and conjugal happiness. But where, oh God tell me, where is the woman? Night and morning I pray for a wife, lovely, beautiful and true; one with whom I may be safe from the snares of temptation; a woman after Thine own heart, the companion of my life and of my mind, and with whom I may raise up children to Thine honour and glory, through Jesus Christ our Lord.

A week or so later he found her. But the manner in which his prayers were answered was surprising and bothersome. Of the 'many amiable girls' he had in view in the summer of 1829, Lady Emily Cowper particularly attracted him. 'She is lovely, accomplished, clever, ladylike, of most modest demeanour, with an air of virgin indifference towards all admirers.' But there was a snag. Her mother's family was *very* Whiggish. Her father was the fifth Earl Cowper; her mother was daughter of that first Viscountess Melbourne who was, during the most splendid years of her bright life, bosom friend of Georgiana, Duchess of Devonshire, and discreet mistress of George Wyndham, third Earl of Egremont; the young Victoria's beloved 'Lord M.' was her cousin. These connexions bothered Ashley. He did his best to be fair, to put it as gently as he could. Her family, he recorded in his diary, was 'gifted with talent and good-humour', but it 'seems to confuse the distinctions between right and wrong'. But would the daughter necessarily go the way of the mother? This question answered itself, and so Lady Emily became a serious candidate. 'I will enquire,' he concluded that great day's entries, 'and I will implore almighty Providence to aid my judgment and direct my choice.'

He saw her again on the 3rd, the 9th and the 10th. By now his affections were wholly engaged, and her worldly-wise mama at any rate must have realized that Emily had a serious suitor. Perhaps Ashley was only another serious suitor. Whether he had precursors or rivals, we cannot be sure. But of one thing we can be perfectly sure: Ashley's courtship was the most curious that any female of that gifted, gay and good-humoured family had ever experienced. For his piety, principles and mild priggishness made him watch Emily like a hawk, analysing every phrase and action for traces of inherited paganism or vice even while his heart succumbed ever more deeply to her

charms. He was assiduous in his attentions, and was clearly
'in love' by the common understanding of the phrase; but,
never adept at dissembling, he appeared just a little too suspicious and superior; his diary seems to suggest that he
wanted her to commit herself to him before he would commit
himself to her; and the consequence was that, as he neared the
conclusion that Emily was providence's choice for him, Emily
and her mama increasingly wondered whether Ashley was the
right choice for them. Her mama was inscrutable. Emily
herself, while perfectly charming, showed him no special
favour. 'Has she any liking for me?' he wondered on the
evening of the 11th. 'I think that there was, yesterday evening,
a character of tenderness in her manner and tone of voice
somewhat unusual, particularly when we were looking at the
distant prospect. . . . How shall I ascertain her feelings? . . .
I feel as though I could love her beyond the love of mortals.
Oh great God, what a treasure to possess such a darling!' By
the 12th he was sure, and was seeking a chance to propose.
Emily could not make up her mind. At first she managed to
fight off a proposal by spoiling his openings as he made them;
but against so determined a suitor such wiles could not work
for long. On the 13th his passion forced her to make some
declaration of her mind.

I said everything to elicit a check, if she were inclined to give one; I
seized her hand repeatedly, I gave every possible sign; she did not
correspond, but she did not *discourage* me; . . . at last I approached
the final question; I made it by a periphrasis, and was, I know not
what, but certainly *not accepted* . . . but still her manner was soft
and tender; 'I have not known you very long,' she said: I became
very angry and irritated . . . she seemed alarmed and entreated me
. . . we walked home; I could not but esteem her decision – it was so
honest and unworldly – her manner then was quite changed, she took
my arm, was lively but tender, was anxious to remain out and, *so
different from the preceding night*, never quitted me once . . . what
am I to understand? Good heavens, she *cannot be averse* to my
proposal! I am altered, I am as a man from whom a fit of drunken-
ness has just passed. . . .

He wondered what to do next. The pain of uncertainty was unbearable. 'I will endeavour to pique her by indifference on my part. I will have recourse to prayer. . . . God eternally bless her!'

The next six weeks were weeks of anguish for Ashley. He was desperately in love. His passion consumed him. His diary deals with nothing else. Minny (for so she had now become) was never nasty to him. Again and again she had the chance to brush him off. She never decisively did so, although he often thought her hard. She must at least have *liked* him. Sometimes she really seemed to love him. But she would not be hurried, and Ashley could not make out why. Sensitive and suspicious, he thought the mother might be to blame. To Ashley she was always quite encouraging: 'Lord Cowper and myself are perfectly favourable – but Minny must make up her own mind – be sure she finds your company most agreeable, yourself very handsome – but remember she is still very young,' and so on. From some of the things that Minny said, Ashley thought that Lady Cowper was not quite as amicable and uninterfering as she claimed to be. If she had pointed out that Ashley had very little to live on; that he was dependent on the goodwill of a notoriously unsympathetic father; that the family estates, to which he would in due course succeed, were heavily burdened with debt; and that his piety, restrained and gentlemanly though it was, might yet indicate a character perverse and difficult – if she had said all this, she would not have gone beyond her maternal duty. Probably she did say all this. Minny could in any case have thought of most of it for herself. She told him that 'she wished to know him better – he puzzled her – they had not known each other long enough'. Now and then she became more explicit. On the 23rd, when he dined with her family: 'Had much conversation at the pianoforte; suffered agonies of torture and vexation; she had *another* doubt, that I was violent in my temper. . . .' Ashley protested that he might be impetuous and enthusiastic but that he was not cruel or violent; she agreed she had no evidence that he was; but still, in a matter so important, she wished to make sure. Next day, it was something else. People had been talking about the affair (indeed it must have been a very conspicuous one!) and not everything they said about Ashley was reassuring: 'He is so enthusiastic, he must be capricious' . . . 'Take care, he has a high sense of religion, he is almost a Saint' (the contemporary hostile nickname for an Evangelical). 'I rejected the last charge,' recorded Ashley, but 'owned the first and said I glory in it; and do you not think, said I, that it is the best guarantee a man can offer? No doubt, she replied in a hearty tone of conviction. . . . I afterwards said, "I have a deep sense of religion, I avow it, but do you see in me any moroseness, any fanaticism, any superstitious excess?" "Oh not at all" . . . .'

So it went on day after day – the young man ardent, tense, urgent and demanding; the lovely girl impressed, flattered, affectionate and often inclining to commit herself to him, but held back both by a reasonable desire to be sure he was himself reasonable and no doubt by prudent parental reminders that Ashley was not the only good fish in the sea. On 16 September he left wherever they were for London. She kept him company for the first seven miles. It was raining but 'she was kind, affectionate and attentive'; he reproached her 'for humming a quadrille at such a moment' but was pacified by her explanation that she did it to hide her feelings; they shook hands at parting, 'and, *for the first time*, SHE pressed mine warmly'. After this, one would have thought Ashley need hardly have doubted the outcome. Lady Cowper, however, would now have Minny all to herself, and Ashley had become convinced she was his enemy. All through life he tended to run to self-pity, and to dramatize situations. He never indulged this tendency more than at this juncture – when his best friends, not to mention his future wife, must have found him exceedingly tiresome.

Oh God my father, what a cruel state of doubt and misery! . . . I have prayed and prayed, and not this day or yesterday but for years that I might attain a virtuous and affectionate wife; here is the woman before me! I cannot easily transfer my heart; but if I fail to secure her, all is lost, and I shall tremble even for my eternal salvation. In marriage I could practise ten thousand virtues which I must, I know too well, omit in celibacy. – Oh God, assist me!

What happened thereafter is not at all clear. Six days later, in London, he wrote: 'I cannot record half of what passes within me; I am wretched to a degree I never yet experienced; if she be a person of heart and character, she must be mine.' Two and a half weeks later, at St Giles's:

... my resolution is taken; never has man been so tortured, insulted: every feeling I have has been toyed with – it seems that I could well make up my mind to quit this life; I almost fear to continue in it – a little time for preparation is all I require – even my own friend Harriet Leveson has lost tenderness and affection in her dealings with me. [Then, added later that day] No, it is not so, *far very far from it* – I have found the contrary, heaven eternally bless her!

A fortnight later: 'I have been much suffering and much praying; the day is at hand to decide my fate. I opened the Book to read the Psalms for the day; the first was the 116th – it encouraged comfort – it seems as if God had prepared a happiness in store for me – I shall soon see.' Thereafter the diary ceases for six months, notes something quite insignificant on 22 March 1830, then ceases for another half-year. By the time he resumed it, in October 1830, he had been Minny's husband for over three months.

Ashley was an eminently domestic man. He who had been starved of family life now sought to steep himself in it. Not everybody who goes through a bad time, or learns after it is over to recognize it as a bad time, devotes his energies to saving others from the same. More common seems the careless response, 'I went through it, why shouldn't you?' From whence exactly Ashley got his nobler attitude is not clear. Perhaps he found his ideal of family life, at once romantic and religious, in the wide reading of his twenties; perhaps he saw something like it among the Cowpers or the Bathursts or others of his friends and relations. But however obscure its roots, its fruits were firm and unshakeable: a determination to give his children a better time than he had had, as well as indulging himself in the paterfamilial joys his father can never have known.

At the heart of this new family was his beloved Minny, whom he loved passionately and to whom he was profoundly devoted. Creevey caught sight of her about the same time as Ashley: 'the leading favourite of the town *so far*', he reported on 3 March 1829. 'She is very inferior to her fame for looks, but very natural, lively, and appears a good-natured young person.'[1] She must also have been (what Creevey was not the man to notice) a fairly serious-minded young person, sufficiently so to convince Ashley that she would prove his ideal soul-mate and to convince herself that she could face life with one so singularly serious. After all, she need not have married him. Her family was not keen on her doing so. She was not yet twenty when she did; she was one of the belles of the season, a bright new star in the central constellation of Whig aristocracy; Ashley was, in wordly terms, no great catch. His goodness and his true nobility of character no less than the urgent passion of his courtship must have helped to shape her choice, just as they probably helped to shape her religious ideas once they were together. However far her piety fell short of the Evangelical extremity of his, it was quite enough to satisfy him; she was a 'wonderful combination of truth, simplicity, joyousness of heart, and purity of spirit,' he told Lady Gainsborough – 'a sincere, sunny and gentle follower of our Lord'.[2] They read the Bible together and conducted the religious education of their children upon an agreed plan. He always noted in his diary, on the many Sundays when he 'took the sacrament', whether Minny had been with him or not; and she always was with him, when she was not away at her mother's with the children. She was Evangelical enough to engage with her dying son Francis in ultra-Evangelical discussion about the Second Advent, comforting him with the information 'that Dr Cumming and others were of opinion that the close of the present dispensation was nearer than was ordinarily calculated by 160 years' (2 June 1849). Nothing in

1 *The Creevey Papers*, ed. H. Maxwell (1904), ii. 198.
2 Hodder, iii. 315.

the manner of her own death worried him, as he was so apt to be worried by unevangelical deaths:

Minny, my own Minny, is gone. God took her soul to Himself at about twelve o'clock this morning. She has entered into her rest, and has left us to feel the loss of the purest, gentlest kindest, sweetest, and most confiding spirit that ever lived. . . . Almost her last words were, 'None but Christ, none but Christ.'

She was herself, however, too strong a character passively to receive her husband's forceful imprint, however much of his temper and cantankerousness she patiently put up with. For all his love of wife and children, he was not at home an absolutely different man from what he was in public. 'How many times have I in my excitable temper said unjust and cruel things to her!' (15 October 1832). They did not always agree about where to live, at any rate during their latter years together. 'It is a sad thing that I and my wife differ so much in some of our tastes. Her whole desire', he noted on 14 September 1865, 'is residence abroad; a great part of mine, to be at home.' She never liked St Giles's.

I have been in possession 15 years, and only 2 summers, and then partially, have I spent in Dorset; and when today I remarked that 'it was but little', I received for an answer that it was 'quite enough'! I do not reject, nay, I like a foreign tour, but I wish to vary it by a residence at home, a journey in Scotland, etc. . . . and some time must, in duty, be given to one's people and one's estate.

In this department, apparently, she had her way; and once, at any rate, her greater common sense compelled her to point out that religious enthusiasm was making him ridiculous. It happened when he was at Broadstairs in the summer of 1841, 'passing a few days happily with my wife and kids'. He was at the time in a state of great excitement about the establishment, following a mainly Prussian initiative, of the Protestant Bishopric of Jerusalem; and evidently Minny got fed up with it.

Never till now have I recorded words however painful [he wrote on Sunday, 22 August 1841]. I do it here as a guide for the future, in sorrow, not in anger. 'You din this perpetually in my ears, and it sets my back up against it, always talking of how wonderful how wonderful' .... (– mocking the manner –) this was an expression of deep thankfulness to Almighty God for His wonderful goodness in inspiring the heart of the King of Prussia; but where is sympathy of feeling, the sweetest comfort under danger and trouble?

Evidently she was very good for him.

They had ten children: six boys and four girls. Ashley was always deeply involved in her sufferings. 'Took the sacrament on Good Friday and Easter Sunday, but poor Minny lay at home confined to the sofa, in danger of a miscarriage' (29 March 1842). Anxiety continued for four months; then – 'At half past twelve on Sunday night Minny was safely delivered of another daughter. By God's great and most undeserved mercy her time was short and even easy – blessed be His holy name!' (25 July 1842). He does not seem to have disliked the sight and sound of babies, although of course he was protected from the more wearing aspect of them by the normal body-guard of nursemaids. And he loved children – all children – in no merely sentimental way. Almost the principal motive behind his philanthropic work was a masterful and magnificent determination to minimize the suffering of children and young persons, to maximise their chances of a secure family life. He tried to make his own home a model of his universal ideal, watching over the 'kids', as he often referred to them, with tender vigilance. As they grew older, they perhaps found his tenderness too anxious, his vigilance too restless. While they were tiny, however, he must have made them a very good father, and theirs was obviously a happy family, with plenty of fun and freedom as well as principle and piety. On Easter Sunday, 1843, they were all at the sea-side. 'Minny and I, through God's mercy, took the sacrament together – had afterwards, towards evening, a solitary walk on the sea-shore (while the blessed children ran about the sands) and recalled the past, and anticipated the future, in faith, and fear, and fervent prayer.' His diary holds many such entries.

They spent a lot of their time with Minny's relations. His parents never wanted to see them; the dust-covers were hardly ever taken off the furniture at St Giles's. Her people were wealthy and welcoming. She liked being back with them, the children had a good time there, and Ashley, religiously though he seems sometimes to have battled against the temptation, found them very pleasant. So, when not at their town house, 49 Brook Street, they were usually either at Panshanger, her parents' house near Hertford, or, after her mother married Lord Palmerston *en secondes noces*, at his beautiful house, Broadlands, near Romsey, in Hampshire.

They also travelled a good deal. At first this was simply for pleasure or as part of the normal aristocratic routine of country-house visiting. One such trip was made in 1839. Ashley, Minny and Antony their eldest boy set out on 9 August by train for Birmingham ('Saw the Bull Ring, famous for mobs and conflagrations . . .'). Then via Liverpool to the Lakes, where he was sorry to miss his admired pen-friend, the leading Tory publicist of the Reform Bill period, Robert Southey. Carlisle he disliked: 'a bad place, and always has been'. At Netherby he was sorry to find no evening service on the Lord's Day: 'I dearly love the afternoon service of a rural parish. Its omission is a great error; the service is good for all, and necessary for many who cannot attend the earlier worship.'

Their first nights in Scotland were spent at Newbattle Abbey, the Marquis of Lothian's house. He was sorry to leave it: 'This is the great drawback in touring; no sooner are you well shaken together, and become at ease, then the tocsin sounds for separation. It is, however, a facsimile of the world itself, and as such should be improved into a moral lesson. . . .' On their first Sunday in Scotland they went 'to Kirk! absolutely the Presbyterian Kirk. What could we do otherwise if we desired to go to any place of worship at all? But they protest against Popery and preach the Atonement in faith and love, so I can, under stress of weather, take shelter in one of their chapels.' But he disliked the form of service – 'I cannot call it worship; it appeals neither to the senses, the feelings, nor the reason' – and although he loved Scotland and revisited it again and again, he never went to the Kirk if there was an acceptable episcopalian church within reach. After Edinburgh,

Linlithgow and the Trossachs, they stayed at Rossie Priory, the home of Lord Kinnaird, another Evangelical peer; then through the Highlands to Oban (his bed was so short there that he was 'like a basket of game – covered in the middle, with head and feet out') and so down the west coast to Glasgow where he hobnobbed with Archibald Alison, the pious and industrious Tory historian – 'A man after my own heart. . . . He takes expanded surveys of past, present and future times . . . sees the first chapters of Genesis in the history of all kingdoms, peoples and nations. He stated beautifully and truly that the democratic principle is anti-Christian [and] plainly discerns the French Revolution in the Apocalypse. . . .'

On the homeward journey they stayed at Chillingham Castle, and had great excitements with the 'wild cattle'.

Sandy – the antlered despot of the park – seems to be the lord and master of Chillingham; he is far more talked about than Lord Tankerville, and in fact there is reason for it, as he puts every one's limbs in danger, and Lord Tankerville threatens none. What with bulls, and what with stags, our lives here are in a constant state of excitement, a pleasing sense of dignified peril. We discuss them by day, and dream of them by night . . . .

After visits to Alnwick and Ravensworth they spent several days with the Vyners at Newby, where he had a noteworthy 'walk with Minny. Much interesting conversation with the darling. It is a wonderful accomplishment, and a most beautiful answer to one's prayers, to have obtained a wife, in the highest matters and the smallest details, after my imagination and my heart. . . .' At Castle Howard, their next stop, he was glad to renew his friendship with the Carlisles. Chatsworth he found almost oppressively grand – 'Everything magnificent, and half of it unnecessary. . . . It is a curious thing to have seen; it is probably the last great effort of hereditary wealth, of aristocratical competition with the splendour of kings.' They moved on to Rowton in Shropshire, where his sister Charlotte lived with her genial husband Henry Lyster; and so back to Brook Street, after more than three months on the move. 'Thus are we all again, once more, together. . . . We looked for health and amusement, we found both; we sought instruction, it has not been wanting; body and mind have been alike strengthened.'

Their first foreign tour was made in 1833, in company with Minny's parents. His travelling journal, elaborate and thoughtful as ever, shows him observant, open-minded, cultivated and receptive. They were in Roman Catholic countries almost all the time. He disliked Popery, but was not blind to its virtues. He liked to see the cross and crucifix so publicly proclaimed, and at Padua even bought a small crucifix, simply to 'recall His death and passion', and to force himself 'to look on Him whom we pierced'. He liked to see the mixing of all social classes in the churches, and he realized that not all of their behaviour in church was just superstitious or profane. 'One great and honourable characteristic of this religion is, as Minny observed to me, that no one is ashamed to exhibit devotion.' Where there was no Protestant place of worship, 'We preferred, to total omission, saying a few prayers in a house dedicated to His Honour and service.' He read a lot of Massillon, but he read Gibbon too. They were indefatigable sight-seers and gallery-goers. He seems to have taken most notice of religious paintings, but any good work of art was liable to catch his interest. In no particular did they depart from the normal course of nobility on a grand tour. They went to operas as well as church-services (Ashley thought the Te Deum at the new year's eve service in the Gesù 'a compound of *Tancredi, Semiramide and Robert le Diable*'), and to several balls ('Minny looked heavenly. . . . Is it wrong to be so entirely proud of, and happy in, one's wife's beauty? But surely there is nothing so pretty and fascinating as my Min') and saw 'nothing but innocence' in the Carnival at Nice, which, with his Gibbon to hand, he learnedly traced back to its heathen origins.

This was his second visit to Italy – the first fell in that obscure period between leaving Oxford and meeting Antoinette.[1] Subsequent foreign tours only once took him south of the Alps, and were never again so light-hearted; they were made in search of his own or his family's health, often involved the

1 Hodder, i. 175.

drinking of much bad-tasting water ('It is the life of a whale!...
a hogshead of the Thames would be quite as effective'), and
he increasingly grudged the time they took. He never much
liked the French – except, of course, their lively little children;
children always attracted him, even French ones. Of Paris,
'that pavilion of Belial', he had, as might be expected, a
conventionally unfavourable idea. He could not help admiring
the Germans. But the Italians captivated him, as they have
always tended to captivate Englishmen.

We abuse them, we despise them, we taunt them with cowardice and
degeneracy; and it may be deserved, and it may be true; but are
they incorrigible, or what has made them such? Have they been well
taught? Have they been well ruled? Scattered, at variance with one
another and oppressed; without place or nation, having little to love
and nothing to respect, without the means of patriotism and loyalty,
what can be demanded of them? Yet consider their genius. . . .
Among so many millions cannot virtue and genius again take root?

He dreamed, as he travelled north towards the fogs and frosts
and parliamentary duties of his homeland, of 'the establishment of a "Kingdom of Italy" ', and he could not quite dismiss
his dream, for all the frightening circumstances of violence and
revolution that seemed the inevitable path to its accomplishment. 'Good can be purchased at too dear a rate, and two
generations must not be sacrificed for the benefit of a third.
Yet if it pleased God to raise Italy from the dead, what a mass
of materials for every work of greatness!' This was in February 1834. From his generous enthusiasm for the Italian people
– a special instance of his general enthusiasm for the principle
of nationality – Ashley never backslided; and God began to
move in mysterious ways – *very* mysterious French ways –
to bring Ashley's dreams to realization, much sooner than he
expected.

These episodes of holidays and domestic bliss show Ashley
at his most relaxed and cheerful. He was not uncommonly
like this during the thirties and early forties. As the years
went by he kept his capacity for easiness and gaiety on an
ever-tighter rein. The sense of fun, the talent for humour,
the delights of random and receptive observation, he never

indeed quite lost. To the very end he was capable of the entertaining narrative and the apt joke which charmed his company or audience and sent them away thinking how *human* he was. And even if he went in less for pleasure himself, there was never any trace of the kill-joy about him. His Sabbatarianism, which was in any case of less than Scottish severity, inevitably made him seem such; he used to go to great pains to clear himself of the charge. He loved to see people happy, especially young people; and if he did prefer to see their happiness contained within the sanctions of religion, it was only because his idea of happiness extended to eternity. His religion was always a joyful one, however much he himself, as he grew older, chose to be gloomy.

For gloomy he undoubtedly became. There were several causes for it. One was simply his ever-growing acquaintance with the quantity and consequences of the sin, squalor and suffering in which humanity was involved; increasingly it haunted him, forbidding the use of time and mind on less momentous things. Another cause lay in his profoundly pessimistic political philosophy. The older he grew, the more time he would spend filling page after page of his diary with quite acute and comprehensive analysis of the present bad state of society, with detailed prophecies of the way it would continue to go from bad to worse. The writing of these passages obviously gave him deep satisfaction. He never got bored going over the same ground again and again, never suspected any inconsistency in affirming the growing badness of a society which he, more than any other Victorian, had not unsuccessfully endeavoured – as he himself in less sombre mood would admit – to make better. He liked the sense of tracing the workings of God's inexorable providence, and he traced it, of course, along his own fundamentalist and ultra-Tory lines. To these intellectual obsessions was added the force of his own habitual tendencies towards melancholy, exaggeration, and self-pity, and (what demands less cursory notice) his financial and family worries. He was not a man to carry troubles lightly; and he certainly had a fair share of them.

Ashley was never well-off. Most peers of his status and abilities would have sought salaried office and improved their finances that way. It was not a way that Ashley felt free to follow, once he had resolved to devote his life to the pursuit of philanthropy and national virtue. He never again held any paid office after his five months at the Admiralty early in 1835. The fifty-odd years of service with the Lunacy Commissioners, the five years of hard labour at the Board of Health, were completely unremunerated. As an English peer and a Christian gentleman, he was expected to give his services freely; and so he gave them, though not without rueful reflections that some of his colleagues in those departments had been paid handsomely for working less hard.

His financial difficulties became acute after his succession to the earldom in 1851.[1] His children were growing up. Antony, indeed, was for the time being nearly self-supporting, in the Navy; Francis had recently died. But there were still four sons to educate, and four girls to provide for. On coming to the estate, he found it in bad shape and indebted for well over £100,000. He sold the Dorchester property for £48,500. To pay off pressing debts he borrowed £52,000 on mortgage from the Hand in Hand Assurance Company. His gross income was about £14,000; but of that £2,000 fell to his mother's share (and she lived on until 1865) – £2,800 went to the Hand in Hand and other lesser mortgagers – and £6,000 to his steward for management, repairs, taxes, rent-charges and so on. This left only a very modest disposable income for an English earl. Yet, with the continued generosity of his in-laws, he might still have jogged along, had not his good-nature and thirst for righteousness soon combined to involve him in desperate difficulties. First, he borrowed another £70,000 to finance the improvement of the estate, 'to advance the condition of the people, to maintain the honour of landed proprietors, and leave the estate to my son with a revenue that I could never touch on my own behalf'. For years his enemies had delighted to point out how wretched, generally, the Dorsetshire peasantry

1 The following account is based largely on the 'Narrative of Property' given in a slim black leather volume in among the diaries.

were, and how those on the Shaftesbury estates were among
the worst off. Shaftesbury had been much galled by these
attacks, which were substantially true; yet there was nothing
he could do to improve matters, so long as his father lived,
beyond to proclaim his ideal of good landlordship – and that,
when he had bravely produced it at a big agricultural dinner
at Sturminster in November 1843, had only led to a frightful
row with his father[1] and the growth of that hostility within
the county which ended his career as its M.P. in 1846. Now at
last he was able, albeit with difficulty, to do something for
the lower orders. Gallantly he did it; but, as it turned out,
imprudently. Too much of the outlay was unproductive; and
its management was in the hands of an unjust steward.

Not the least of Shaftesbury's debts to Palmerston was his
first serious warning that his agent, Waters, was probably a
crook. Shaftesbury had no idea of this. His London solicitors,
Nichol and Burnett, had actually told him to leave everything
to Waters as his father had done. He had been glad enough to
do so. But at the end of November 1861 Palmerston wrote him
a wonderfully tactful, kind and helpful letter, saying that
people had been talking about all Shaftesbury's lavish improvements and the agent in charge of them: 'If report says
true, he at one time kept race-horses and brood mares, and
was connected with racing men, and, of course, was a betting
man; all these things, if they do not lead a man astray, infuse
into his mind habits of restlessness not very suitable to accurate economy.' Why not get Nichol and Burnett to send
someone to Dorset and find out exactly what was going on?

Shaftesbury at once did so; and soon it became horribly
clear, not only that Waters had defrauded him of many
thousands of pounds, but that his solicitors had been almost
criminally negligent. The auditors to whom they had entrusted
the auditing of Waters's accounts – Burnett, Newman and
Co.! – had never demanded proper statements from Waters,
never checked them against the bank books, had 'first delayed,
. . . then hurried through the accounts, . . . because they were
always so intricate, confused and unintelligible'. *Quis custodiet*

1 See below, p. 112.

ipsos custodes? Shaftesbury was learning the hard way that experts cannot always – not even when they are London professional men – be trusted. In the summer of 1863 he sacked Waters, and soon afterwards instituted legal proceedings against him. This turned out to be unwise. The merits of the case, which came to court in March 1866, cannot now be ascertained. Its progress cast Shaftesbury into the depths. 'This unrighteous judge', he wrote on the evening of the first day, 'has prejudged the case, and, being alike stupid and malignant, he will listen to nothing in my favour.' Waters, he believed, after years of deliberate obfuscation of the facts, was now perjuring himself. The humiliations of defeat, or being made publicly to look silly, and of having over-confidently assumed that God was on his side, must have hurt more even than the thought of all that money down the drain. On 19 March 1866:

My state is one of amazement. My defeat and dishonours are founded on the most fearful perjuries; and the unholy attestation of that great name, in which I have ever trusted has been the means of my ruin. Will not God assert His own honour, and His own commandment, and bestow some public proof that the invocation of His name is yet . . . a mainstay and an assurance to human society?

It puzzled him that such a good cause, supported by 'so many ardent, continuous faithful prayers – such earnest supplications to be guided, delivered, saved from sorrow and disgrace', should have gone wrong. Could they have been praying on the other side too? Despite his grief and perplexity, he fought on. So did Waters, whose friends raised a subscription for him (Shaftesbury thought the Puseyites had taken him up!). The wretched business dragged on until mid-1868. Shaftesbury's friends then prevailed on him to accept a settlement out of court, with Lord Portman as arbitrator. It left him, he reckoned, £5,000 the poorer.

This painful but necessary review of Shaftesbury's private troubles may be brought to a close with a glance at his relations with his children. Four of them died before their father: Francis, his favourite, in 1849, when he was sixteen; Maurice, who seems to have been epileptic, aged twenty, in 1855; Mary in 1861, Constance in 1872. These losses, of course, grieved him deeply. Yet they seem to have grieved him less, over the course of time, than the gulf that separated him from Antony, his eldest. His grief at their deaths was susceptible of religious consolation; from his grief at 'Accy's' manner of life, there was no such relief. How far he was himself to blame for the rift that came between them can only be guessed. Probably, like Prince Albert and so many other fond fathers before and since, he watched over his son and heir's growth all too tenderly, and made him obstinate rather than responsive. Probably, also, Accy was not so bad as his disappointed father thought. Whether he was or not, however, made no difference to Shaftesbury's state of mind; which the contemplation of Accy's doings brought often to despair.

Antony went to an Evangelical boarding-school on the Isle of Wight in the autumn of 1843. 'During many years', recorded his father on the eve of his going (30 October 1843), 'I have passed every morning with him, hearing and reading the Word of God. ... I have watched every moment, weighed every expression, considered every thought, and seized every opportunity to drop a word in season. ...' Perhaps the boy found school rather a relief. (But Francis and Evelyn apparently took to this sort of thing like ducks to water). Two years later he went to Rugby. His parents wrote continually to him. Antony's replies, which from his first school had been 'blessed', now became 'unsatisfactory. He shuns answers to our queries about religion and prayers; he passes altogether without notice my entreaties and exhortations. I must go there and spend a day ...' (17 September 1845). Antony was not clever enough for Oxford, so in 1848 he went into the Navy. His parents went to Portsmouth to see him off on H.M.S. *Havannah* for a three-year cruise. 'I see him now; I shall see him for ever till we meet again, standing at the shipside, and watching us depart. Oh, Christ, our only Saviour and Redeemer, have mercy on the lad in body and soul. ...' He wrote home as often as could have been expected, and always very pleasantly; but still he gave no sign of that religious 'seriousness' they yearned for. In 1851 he was home safely, and they all had Christmas together – all, that is, save Francis, who had been 'the jewel, the crown of the family. . . . Read to them I Thess. iv from 9 to end, and offered prayer. Was Antony touched or not?' (25 December 1851). Apparently not. He was soon off again, to the Baltic; but his manner of life, at sea or at home, left more and more to be desired. 'No news yet of Antony', on 16 June 1854; 'but, as it is said, "coming events cast their shadows before", so the arrival of bills and heavy demands indicate pretty clearly his present and future life. . . . Meanwhile [Shaftesbury's financial troubles were thickening just now] as Peel used to say, I have three courses. . . .' Four days later: 'No, I find that I have not even one. I am at my wit's end. . . .'

A year or so later Antony was out of the Navy. He had not done well enough to earn promotion. 'Alas, alas, there is one thing he can do, and but one – he can and will ruin me, himself, and the family; and convert the ancient acres of St Giles's into top-boots, cigars, jewellery, and all the para-phernalia of profligate and useless life' (6 February 1855). After a spell as a man about town he married Harriet, daughter of the third Marquess of Donegal. Shaftesbury hoped she would influence him for good, since his parents could not; whatever her effect on him, it brought his father no great comfort. When a son was born, in 1869, and St Giles's was gay with traditional festivities, Shaftesbury thought he could for a moment see in Antony his ideal of a resident, popular, aristocratic landowner. But it was only wishful thinking, of the kind to which his generous emotions often led him. An-tony and Harriet spent neither Christmas nor New Year's Day at home, sending 'a series of wretched and forged excuses' (31 December 1869); they sacked their pious governess and replaced her with a more fashionable foreigner – 'perhaps a covert jesuit or an open infidel' (31 January 1870); and Shaftesbury was too disillusioned to pretend even to himself that his son would be a proper person to stand for the county, as his cronies were urging him to do. There seems to have been no recovery of affection between them. It was to Evelyn ('Edy') and his wife 'Sissey', to his daughter Victoria ('Vea') and her husband Lord Templemore, and to his unmarried daughter Edith, that the old man looked for love and company in his declining years.

Exeter Hall in 1843

2

THE AFFLICTED IN MIND

LORD SHAFTESBURY'S work in connexion with mental illness, although his biographers have hardly been able to ignore it, seems never to have been given the place it merits. This is probably because Shaftesbury himself became much more excited about other of his good works, the prosecution of which was apt to send up much more noise and flame. His excitement has communicated itself to his biographers, and so the cause for which he worked the longest, in which he was the most singular and isolated, has been left rather on one side. Yet there is a case for regarding it as his noblest achievement. It shows him at his very best – painstaking, selfless, efficient, intelligent, sensitive, humble, humane. From this cause he could derive none of those sentimental gratifications – the converted costermonger's confession, the salvaged flower-girl's gratitude – which sweetened his contacts with rightminded sufferers. It was not a work that won him great glory or popular acclaim; and there were elements in Shaftesbury that sought such things. It was, as far as we can tell, most valuable and enlightened work; the several disputes in which he had to participate show him on the side approved by modern mental science. It demonstrated very clearly those talents for business – clear-headedness, mastery of detail, ability to delegate without discarding responsibility – which could have taken him to high political office. And, for all its thanklessness and obscurity, he stuck to it for nearly sixty years. It was his first substantial philanthropy, forced upon him as an uncomfortable and painful burden – 'nothing poetical' about it, as he grimly remarked on 13 November 1828 – which he could not in good conscience refuse to take up, and in its behalf he made his first important speech in Parliament. This was in February 1828, when he seconded Robert Gordon's motion to bring in two Bills based on the report of the Select Committee he had just been on. The Bills became law, and Ashley became a member of the Metropolitan Lunacy Commission thereby established. From 1829 he acted as its chairman. Its work extended to cover the whole nation in the early forties and in 1845 it was replaced by a permanent Lunacy Commission, with Ashley as its permanent chairman. He stayed there till he died.

The word 'lunacy' has almost vanished from our language. Nowadays we prefer to speak of mental illness, implying a wide range of mental disturbances, from the temporary and trivial on one side to the permanent and deep-rooted on the other, all, however, susceptible to treatment of some kind and most of them ultimately remediable. Mental illness has been brought under the same cover as physical. What was regarded before the nineteenth century as a mysterious, painful and unavoidable working of God's providence, has become viewed as not necessarily the less God's providence but as an aspect of the human condition capable of alleviation through several of the blessings which only modern man enjoys: more exact science, more abundant wealth, larger potentialities of improvement, and hence further-reaching notions of charity than were possible earlier on. Ignorance, false shame, cruelty and parsimony still indeed baulk improvement in the lot of a class of unfortunates about whom it is peculiarly easy to feel impatience and irritation. Shaftesbury's work is by no means yet completed.

When Shaftesbury first interested himself in lunatics, their condition was horrible, as it had been since the beginning of time. How well or badly treated they were depended partly on the nature of their malady, partly on their social class. Violent and dangerous lunatics were generally confined; chained up in beastly solitude in dark out-houses or cellars, or viewed as malefactors, locked up in gaol, flogged, tortured, handled with maximum brutality. The socially harmless might be better off. If of the lower orders of society, they often roamed about on the loose, did odd jobs for nothing, learnt the hard way whose paths to keep out of, and shared the modest amenities of the workhouse with the rest of the flotsam and

jetsam of their society. If of the middling or upper classes,
however, they might not get along so well. At all levels of
society, of course, a larger latitude of behaviour was then
taken for granted than either convention or the law now
permits. Deeds and words that would, by our more squeamish
standards, clamour for psychiatric treatment or doom their
demonstrator to social isolation were apt to be viewed merely
as legitimate eccentricities, or as particularly strong marks of
character. To that extent, society then managed its misfits
better than we do. But once the line of legitimate eccentricity
was crossed, or whenever a family (socially climbing perhaps,
and desperate to appear 'respectable') believed that no eccentricity was permissible, the middle or upper class lunatic
was in trouble no less bad – sometimes even worse – than that
which beset his lower-born brethren. Those who had the means
to keep their mad relation out of sight could easily do so; he
might be locked up at home, in an attic or secret room, or
sent away to a keeper or a private madhouse; and from being
out of sight, it was no distance at all for an unwanted, embarrassing, helpless human being to falling out of mind. To
whom could he appeal? No one would listen, no judge would
(in the unlikely event of his having friends to bring his case
before a judge) grant him a habeas corpus; the man was mad!
It was as difficult for the victim of such a system, once labelled
mad, to prove he was not so, as for a woman once brought
before the courts of sixteenth-century Bamberg or seventeenth-
century Salem on a charge of witchcraft to prove she was not
a witch; and, of course, many of its victims were not mad at all
– to begin with, anyway. They might just be odd, or neurotic;
or (and it was this that gave the system its most sinister
aspects) they might simply be *inconvenient*, standing in the
way of desirable marriage or a profitable sale, thwarting some
strong man's will, or posing some awkward question. For such
inconvenient people, if they were weak or imprudent, the
madhouse was a much simpler solution than murder.

Into this shadowy system of horror and inhumanity a little
light began to penetrate during the latter years of the eighteenth
century. Every aspect of human wretchedness was then being

looked at with an eye to its alleviation, and the views of the newly intelligent and optimistic experts were beginning to receive the support (without which their sphere of action was bound to stay small) of a newly sensitive and humane public. Lunatics were looked at as well as slaves, paupers, prisoners and schoolchildren; and medical science collaborated with Christian conscience to point the way to better things. In France it was Pinet, in America Rush and Bond; in England William Tuke, who showed at the York 'Retreat' how the mentally sick could be cared for, and even cured, without the mechanical restraints and savage physical treatments that were *de rigueur* in London's Bethlem Hospital and the few other institutions that offered some sort of medical attention as well as incarceration. From the Tukes at York (there were three generations of them) this humane light spread, mixing as it went with a new readiness to take an interest and a growing sense of responsibility, which the Select Committees of 1763, 1808, and 1814–15, and the statutes following them in 1774, 1808 and 1819, feebly reflected. But little progress had been made before Ashley got involved. A few counties had built asylums, but how they ran them was their own business; the weak machinery for the inspection of private madhouses was practically useless; the Lord Chancellor and the Royal College of Physicians divided and diluted between them what scanty central authority there was; while the wretched 'single patients', of whom there were none knew how many, remained totally uncared for. The York 'Retreat' showed the right way to approach the question, but a series of horrific scandals and revelations about other asylums showed how little likelihood there was of the Tukes's lead being followed without authoritative guidance and pressure.

This guidance and pressure was first made available under Robert Gordon's Acts of 1828. They gave the Home Secretary a general oversight over all institutions, public or private. This control he would exercise through the agency of visiting committees of magistrates throughout the provinces, and the fifteen Metropolitan Lunacy Commissioners, whose business it was to licence, to inspect – with or without notice, even at

dead of night if malpractices had been alleged upon oath –
and, if they thought fit, to order the release of persons from
the many private asylums in the greater London area. Ashley
was one of these, and of course he was one of the most active.
The work was rigorous and harrowing. Conditions in many
of the licensed houses thus for the first time exposed to view
were often repulsive. By means of nocturnal and Sunday
visits, Ashley and his colleagues saw them at their darkest
and worst, and enforced improvements by threatening to
have their licences revoked. But that extreme remedy was
reserved for the incorrigible. The Commissioners preferred to
work gently, by persuasion; which was moreover the politic
course to take, firstly because there was as yet little suitable
accommodation waiting to receive those set at large by clo-
sures, and secondly because the medical profession was (as it
still is) largely uninterested in and ignorant concerning mental
illness, and the proprietors of the licensed houses – usually
doctors themselves – could amass plenty of apparently 'expert' evidence to justify all but their more gross and ghastly
shortcomings.

Ashley early acquired a deep suspicion of these proprietors,
which only began to wear off in the sixties. What principally
worried him was that they had a financial interest in keeping
their houses full. They could no longer very easily detain *sane*
people, because the Commissioners (or, in the provinces, the
visiting magistrates, who might, however, be susceptible to
local influence) could, and frequently did, order the release of
such; but they could refrain from curing the palpably insane.
No doubt some did so. The inducements to retain persons
whose relations paid handsomely and had, so often, no desire
to be bothered with them outside, were very strong. Against
these sinister interests, Ashley and the enlightened fractions of
the medical profession and the humanitarian public (Quakers
were from the start prominent) pitted, first, the greater success
of the new methods of treatment compared with the old, and
second, an appeal to the public to take a more open and calm
view of the question. Although Ashley's official writ only ran
in the metropolitan area, he took a lively interest in progres-

sive asylums (with Dr Connolly's Hanwell at their head after 1839), visited them, studied their reports, and lost no opportunity to recommend the adoption of their methods. He quickly became an expert on the subject; no other British layman, probably, knew as much about it. But it was easier to promote a more enlightened state of affairs behind the asylum walls than to induce in the public a more enlightened state of mind.

One of Ashley's greatest virtues was a readiness to face up to certain uncomfortable facts, and, in dealing with them, to accept uncomfortable consequences. All his philanthropic works were the fruit of this dutiful marriage of perception and response. Poverty, disease, criminality, ignorance, pain, were social facts the recognition of which was apt positively to diminish the *douceur de vivre* of those who lived above them; but to Ashley and his fellow workers they were facts from which conscience allowed them no escape. Now, 'lunacy' was a peculiarly uncomfortable fact, which even the most charitable and philanthropic were liable to blink. Anyone who has come across cases of mental illness or deficiency knows it to be so. A disordered or damaged body is an ailment palpably, sensibly, afflicting, and to even the uninstructed mind fairly intelligible; the cause is clear and physical, the effect clear and lamentable; the sufferer is able to understand his trouble, and co-operate with those who wish to help him. How different is not the case of the disordered or damaged in mind! – The cause invisible and mysterious, the effect confused and troublesome, the sufferer usually incapable of understanding what is wrong with him and apt to make things difficult for potential helpers. Not only are patience, sympathy and understanding sorely tested; neighbours whisper, passers-by jeer or flee; superstition, ignorance and plain human folly and wickedness combine to cast a shadow of suspicion and horror over the whole of the victim's circle. Perhaps society is a little more enlightened and humane than it used to be; it is certainly not as much better as it ought to be in these respects, considering the means at its disposal, than it was in Ashley's lifetime. He wanted to break open the shell of silence. false shame and

selfish indifference that enveloped the subject, to bring
people to recognize, in what they tried to flee from as 'lunacy',
a form of illness or affliction like any other, a particularly
tragic one that demanded love and courage and social acceptance, instead of coldness, squeamishness and seclusion. The
'respectability' that first tried not to recognize mental illness,
and then tried to hush it up as something disgraceful or
unnatural, seemed to him absolutely immoral and un-
Christian, and whenever occasion offered – in parliamentary
debate, witnessing before committees of inquiry, addressing
interested societies – he did his best to enlighten it.

Part of the explanation of his constant, patient and genuin-
ely humble devotion to the cause lies, probably, in that capacity for introspective self-knowledge which told him how near
he himself could be taken to the uncertain line between what
his age called 'sanity' and 'insanity' by certain of his own mental characteristics – his melancholic self-pity, his irritable
sensitivity, and his equal and alternating suspiciousness and
gullibility. His family history (like most such, when truth is
told) could show examples of the line transgressed; the second
Earl, at any rate, had been weak-minded; his son Maurice's
intellectual development had, he knew, been grievously
impaired by a 'terrible succession of fits', and his eldest son
may (I can find no evidence one way or the other) have shown
early signs of that lack of mental balance which led him to
take his own life in 1886. Moreover, Ashley recognized, more
clearly than anyone could who would not face the question
objectively, charitably and bravely, that a man might be technically 'insane' and yet, not only quite harmless, but even
spiritually gifted. He thought Maruice was. His judgment
may here have been swayed by a father's fondness; but no
one would deny that he was correct in thinking the same about
the poet Cowper.

The speeches in which he commended the cause of the
mentally afflicted to Parliament were among his finest. At his
worst when exercising the religious bees in his bonnet or when
playing upon popular emotions, he was at his very best when

pleading the less popular causes of the helpless and neglected – compassionate yet curiously unsentimental, grave and religious without flatness or cant. Often long and elaborate, his speeches were solidly built and finely proportioned, moving easily from topical examples and legislative or administrative detail to general principle and policy. The perorations of two of his lunacy speeches are particularly notable, as summaries of his attitude to this great question, no less than as illustrations of his attitude to life in general. The first was made in 1844. For two years Ashley and his Metropolitan Commissioners had been busy investigating the state of all the lunatic asylums, public and private, of England and Wales. Now the report was completed. It was the first of its kind, a necessary preliminary to the extension of public control; and Ashley called the Common's attention to it on 23 July. He ended thus:

These unhappy persons are outcasts from all the social and domestic affections of private life – nay, more, from all its cares and duties – and have no refuge but in the laws. You can prevent, by the agency you shall appoint, as you have in many cases prevented, the recurrence of frightful cruelties; you can soothe the days of the incurable, and restore many sufferers to health and usefulness. For we must not run away with the notion that even the hopelessly mad are dead to all capacity of intellectual or moral exertion – quite the reverse; their feelings, too, are painfully alive. . . . Their condition appeals to our highest sympathies, 'Majestic, though in ruin'; for though there may be, in the order of a merciful Providence, some compensating dispensation which abates within, the horrors manifested without, we must judge alone by what we see; and I trust, therefore, that I shall stand excused, though I have consumed so much of your valuable time, when you call to mind that the motion is made on behalf of the most helpless, if not the most afflicted, portion of the human race.

His speech was well received and the Home Secretary told him that he would be given full government support if he would promote legislation next session. ('Prodigious work! but cannot refuse to lighten the burden on a Minister's shoulder. . . . Oh that I might prosper and do something for those desolate and oppressed creatures!' – 21 November 1844). In June

1845 he introduced a brace of Bills, the main points of which were to compel the erection of asylums by the many counties which had not yet done so, and to establish a permanent Lunacy Commission with six salaried members (three doctors and three lawyers) as well as five unpaid (of whom he was to be one, and chairman of the whole), and with powers regularly to inspect *all* licensed institutions at least twice a year, certificated 'single patients' in private houses once a year;[1] at the same time the form of certificate was made more elaborate and rogue-proof. Ashley in concluding his speech begged the Commons to reflect humbly that they were, in a sense, legislating for themselves.

It is our duty and our interest too [he said] when we have health and intellect, . . . leisure and opportunity, to deliberate upon these things before the evil days come, and the years of which we shall say we have no pleasure in them. Here we are sitting in deliberation today; tomorrow we may be subjects of this fearful affliction. Causes, as slight apparently as they are sudden, varying through every degree of intensity . . . will do the awful work, and then 'Farewell, King!' The most exalted intellects, the noblest affections, are transformed into fatuity and corruption, and leave nothing but the sad though salutary lesson – how frail is the tenure by which we hold all that is precious and dignified in human nature.

No other lunacy legislation during Shaftesbury's lifetime was as important as this of 1845. His Commissioners' powers became of course extended as time went by, and their labours only grew heavier, as public asylums multiplied, insane paupers were brought under inspection, and the responsibility for inspection of all classes of patient came to rest increasingly upon them. Shaftesbury's main business became the weekly board meetings. He continued to visit in person, but, after about 1850, only on special occasions, when some grave

1 Ashley and two others constituted a private, secret committee for this latter purpose. They found it far too difficult to do properly and in 1853 the Commission proper was put in charge, as ideally it should have been from the first. But all the same, 1845 marked a great step forward. The slight regulation of single patients intended by the Act of 1829 was easily and regularly evaded. See Shaftesbury's evidence to the 1859 Select Committee (Parliamentary Papers, 1859, iii. 75ff.), Qs. 272ff.

scandal was reported, or some particularly delicate or difficult case called for investigation.

Scandals of the worst old kind virtually disappeared by the middle of the century, although ignorant and excitable readers of Charles Reade's *Hard Cash* might gather that they still persisted in 1863. Into that book (based mainly on examples from the 1820s and 1830s) was crammed every dark indictment imaginable by a quick-working sensational novelist and a public quick to believe every tale of improper certification and unjust confinement with which the newspapers and popular politicians regularly regaled them. The public's attitude was changing. From being able to rely on public opinion to support them, Shaftesbury and his colleagues found they had more and more to stand up against it, and answer its often hysterical charges. Twice the House of Commons set up select committees of inquiry, in 1859 and 1877. Shaftesbury was necessarily the chief witness each time. In 1859 his examination took three days: 922 questions, often answered at great length. In 1877 he got off with 412 questions, over two days. His mastery of the whole subject was not less remarkable than the firmness with which he defended his board's principles of action, and the point of view he shared with the still small number of doctors who were prepared to take mental illness seriously. The battle he waged was, largely, that of the doctors and the social workers against the lawyers and the general public. Shaftesbury sought an end to the old-fashioned, superstitious, ignorant, hypocritical attitude towards mental illness, which, by hushing it up, and by viewing treatment in mental hospitals (often, necessarily, by way of certification) as shameful, too often succeeded only in preventing that early treatment which alone could in most cases effect a cure. The same attitude also, naturally, failed to distinguish properly between the mentally ill and the mentally defective. He thought that the danger lay no longer in getting the wrong people into asylums but rather in keeping the right people out. Occasional mistakes there were bound to be, but they would fade away in proportion as the public became more enlightened and as the medical profession learnt more about mental medicine; the vigilance of his central board, by its quick response to special cases as well as by its regular inspections, would sufficiently deal with mistakes in certification. The lawyers and the public sought to make the conditions for certification so strict that mistakes could not occur, and refused to see in the mental defectives a special class requiring special provision. Shaftesbury and the doctors lost. The burdens of his last years were augmented by a series of attempts to alter the law in the lawyers' direction. Gallantly – for his strength was now ebbing fast, and his voice was reported as weak – he still opposed them. Only eighteen months distant from death, he made one of his last painful appearances in the House of Lords and, unsupported, turned at bay upon the assembled legal peers (at that time much excited by the case of eccentric Georgiana Weldon), giving them a shrewd knock by declaring his belief that there were 'fewer cases of mistake in placing patients under care and treatment than of miscarriages of justice in courts of law'. The 1877 Committee had found only six or seven certificates that needed to be looked at out of the 185,000 issued since 1859, and on close inspection each had been found good. He reviewed the progress made since 1828. It was immense, immeasurable; and it had been achieved by Parliament's delegating some power of binding and loosing to his Lunacy Commissioners and, under them, the doctors. He did not deny that the liberty of the subject was an important issue. He merely thought the subject's sanity mattered too. Early treatment was all-important.

He spoke in the interests of the patient, for whom a cure thus became comparatively easy, and in the interest of the world at large also, who had a deep concern in the abatement of that terrible disorder. The impediments were grave and numerous already – the reluctance of parents and relatives to see, and then believe, the first symptoms of a disturbed intellect; the serious step of consulting a medical man on the point, even though he were the physician of the family; the fear lest anything should transpire, and the public be admitted in any way to the sad secret; all these feelings postponed the final decision, until by long continuance the affection had become almost hopelessly confirmed. . . . The error which led to the confinement of the patient might inflict, though the patient was speedily removed, the taint of supposed insanity; but the error which denied the necessity of it might inflict a greater harm, and fix on the patient the malady for ever. . . .[1]

It was a fine effort, but it cut no ice. The lawyers, brutally aided by Lord Salisbury, beat him down; and soon after his death they won their point, and passed the Act of 1890 which, says the historian of the lunacy laws, 'was to hamper the progress of the mental health movement for nearly seventy years'.[2]

1 5 May 1884: *Hansard*, 3rd series, cclxxxvii. 1271ff.
2 Kathleen Jones, *Mental Health and Social Policy 1845–1959* (1960), p. 40.

3

CHURCH, STATE AND EMPIRE

LORD SHAFTESBURY claimed, with much justice, to be 'an Evangelical of the Evangelicals'. By this he meant that his Evangelical beliefs, once he had acquired them, were fixed, unshakeable, adamantine; that he was not conscious of failing to lead the sort of life that he believed a good Evangelical should; and that he was not just an Evangelical of the Established Church. His faith mattered immensely to him. Indeed one could say that it mattered to him more than anything else, inasmuch as it provided the conscious frame for all his thoughts and his only shelter from an otherwise unbearable certainty of eternal damnation. It was his refuge and his strength. Yet to say that it mattered more to him than anything else might be misleading, inasmuch as such a high valuation, such constant consciousness, of religion often withdraws men from the world into closed sects or religious orders. With Shaftesbury it was quite otherwise. His religion kept him in a state of constant involvement with the world, and his religious meditation, profound and elaborate though it often was, directed him all the time to look outwards into the world where God's grace and providence were at war with man's sin and folly, and to participate in that momentous conflict.

One of the many meditative passages from his diary reveals the spiritual principles that underlay this incessant outward-looking.

Oct. 11th 1857. Read in afternoon Matt. XXV. What a revelation of the future judgment on the largest portion of the human race! Those on the left hand are condemned, not for murder, robbery, debauchery, not for breaches of the Decalogue, or for open blasphemy, not for sins they have *committed*, but for duties they have *ommitted*. And is not this the state of the great mass of mankind? The great mass do not commit great crimes; did they so, society would fall to pieces in the twinkling of an eye; but they go on day after day to their life's end, thinking of themselves, very little of others, and nothing of God. . . . 'I have done no harm', 'I am not worse than my neighbours', 'I have merely used my own', etc. etc.; all these are the pleas, the hopes, the justifications of the 'innocent' world. But while man takes one view. God takes another.'Have you done good? "Have you attempted it?' 'Have you sought to advance my Name?' 'Have you laboured for the physical and spiritual welfare of your fellow sinners?' St James (ib. 17) condenses the spirit of our Lord's words, 'Therefore to him that knoweth to do good and doeth it not, to him it is sin.'

His was an activist as well as a meditative faith; and he was the more at liberty actively to participate in the affairs of the world for being intensely un-ecclesiastical, and indeed quite anti-clerical. No particular concern for any particular visible Church complicated his view of the good Christian's necessary place in society and politics; he preferred the Church of England to any other, but on grounds of expediency and habit rather than principle, and mainly because he valued establishment so highly. The Church of England was established, and it was satisfactorily Protestant; he never needed to think more closely about it than how to keep it so; and no more than any visible Church could it be by definition the Church of Christ, which he understood as the company of all who trusted faithfully in Christ's atonement for their sins, a company drawn out of all visible churches, even the Roman. For the Church in this Evangelical sense, indeed, he would fight to the death. But it was not in its nature such a Church as to induce in its servants any specially ecclesiastical state of mind, or to require them to make 'churchy' distinctions. Its membership was diffused throughout the religious world, just as the religious world was immersed in the world at large. So Shaftesbury, Evangelical of the Evangelicals that he was, had few exclusively, other-worldly, religious concerns. *All* his concerns were religious, and all involved him in those social and political affairs which he believed ought to reflect, at the institutional level, the religious interests of mankind, and could be, in a sense, redeemed like man himself. A nation could be righteous as well as an individual, and a righteous nation could promote God's glory far more splendidly than any less significant association of individuals, no matter how righteous. The vision of a nation forged by Evangelical faith into an instrument for God's use was one which peculiarly attracted Ashley, and contributed to keep his outlook international no less than domestic, general as well as particular. He rose from prayer or Bible study ready and eager to serve the Lord equally by local charity or imperial politics, and never felt any qualitative difference between them.

It is often loosely implied that he was an Evangelical all his life. He was not. His language, his reading, his way of life, his public activities during the later twenties, though perfectly compatible with serious religion, were not those of a committed Evangelical; and moreover he explicitly denied being one when taxed with it by Minny in the summer of 1829.[1] But he became an Evangelical five years later. We do not know exactly how, or when, he became so. Unlike some Evangelicals, he did not subsequently delight to specify the time or means of his conversion. Perhaps it was gradual over a period of weeks or months, the product of prayer and reading, without external help.[2] Perhaps Alexander M'Caul or Edward Bickersteth had something to do with it; they were the clergymen with whom he was most closely connected during the later thirties. Perhaps the new domestic experiences of marriage and parenthood, or the excitements and anxieties of the Reform Bill time, were partly responsible; how seriously he was taking politics just then, is most clearly to be seen in his very solemn and portentous correspondence with the old Tory publicist Robert Southey. However obscure the causes of his conversion, and however gradual its course, it was thorough when it came; and the evidence of his diary suggests that it came during the summer of 1834, when he began to look (vainly) for symptoms of 'awakened religion' in the Tory leaders – when he rejoiced to 'profess his belief' at the Hertford S.P.C.K.

1 See above, p. 26.
2 This is what Hodder implies, in his single brief reference to the matter, i. 197.

meeting – and when he was making the correct party responses to William Roberts's edifying *Memoirs of Hannah More*.

His becoming a fully fledged Evangelical seems not to have materially altered his way of life, for he was already conspicuously Christian; nor did it make him more philanthropic than he already was. He was already devoted to the cause of the mentally ill, committed to that of the mill-workers. He was to take on no notable new social causes for five or six years. But he did take up several new religious causes, and in so doing established his title to succeed to William Wilberforce's proud position, as the leading lay Evangelical of the day.

His first distinctively Evangelical association was the Church Pastoral Aid Society, which sprouted off the main stem of the Church Missionary Society early in 1836. Its main business was to 'extend the means of Grace in and to necessitous parishes . . . by increasing the number of working clergymen in the Church of England, and encouraging the appointment of pious and discreet laymen as helpers to the clergy in duties not ministerial'. The extension of the parochial ministry was something which few serious churchmen did not by then desiderate; but there were ways and ways of doing it. High Churchmen (i.e. those who thought the Evangelicals talked too much about justification by faith alone, too little about the sacraments of baptism and the Eucharist, too familiarly about the mysteries of the Godhead, too disparagingly of the Roman Catholics, and too disrespectfully of episcopacy) particularly disliked this introduction into a nominally Church of England society of the device of lay agency, which had hitherto been used only by Dissenters, and off which all but the wildest Evangelicals had so far shied. It tended, they thought, to the destruction of those formal barriers which should separate the Establishment from its enemies, and it was bound to make still greater the difficulties which bishops already experienced in keeping their subordinates' teaching within the limits of the Thirty-nine Articles. The clergy were not, at that date, easy to discipline. A parson secure in his freehold could carry on pretty much as he pleased, anyway, and the only hold a bishop could commonly exercise over an

incumbent was an economic one. Most urban parishes –
and it was of course to such that the C.P.A.S. was looking –
were very badly off. Bishops and their officials naturally had a
considerable say in the distribution of the diocesan charities
and funds; Parliament had given them considerable discre-
tionary powers to limit the holding of livings in plurality
(which under some circumstances could be innocent enough),
to enforce residence and the building of residence-houses, and
to compel the employment of curates. By the use of such
powers bishops could put the screw on poor clergymen who
declined to follow the prescribed episcopal line, which for
obvious disciplinary and establishmentarian reasons tended
to be the High Church one even when a bishop was not himself a committed High Church man. (As Shaftesbury himself
put it on 31 October 1846, when discussing the state of the
Church with Lord John Russell: 'Through human infirmity,
bishops in general inclined to High Church rather than Low,
and would be blind to many Tractarian tendencies in one who
exalted the episcopal office.') But how could a bishop hold
economic terrors over a clergyman whose supplies came
from an independent source? Such supplies the C.P.A.S.
now promised to provide. They would subsidize Evangelical
incumbents (not that this was new as an Evangelical activity),
help them to pay Evangelical curates, and moreover finance
the employment of a novel class of domestic missionaries,
enthusiastic Evangelical laymen almost bound to be drawn
from the lower classes, laymen over whose activities the bishop
could have practically no control. At the first meetings of the
C.P.A.S. the higher churchmen, whose anxieties about
popular irreligion had attracted them to a society founded to
combat it, stuck out for subsidizing men in orders only.
Finding themselves in a minority, they walked out, and
helped to found the Additional Curates Society a year later.

Ashley was the leading figure in the C.P.A.S. from its
foundation to the end of his life. Regularly in the chair at its
annual general meetings, he used to take the opportunity to
review the current state of the Church and to vent whatever
strong feelings he currently had about it. The C.P.A.S.

meant a lot to him, and chiefly, it would seem, because of his whole-hearted approval of the principles on which it was founded. He admitted no distinction or difference between the capacities of the layman and the clergyman to spread the Gospel, and he was not obsessed with an anxiety to make sure that those who heard the Gospel should hear it in terms which would make them communicant members of the Church of England. Moreover, he believed the essential message of the Gospel to be so simple, that it could often be better conveyed to simple lower-class folk by men of their own social and intellectual levels. This was to go beyond the principles of the C.P.A.S. to those of a similar organization founded about the same time, the London City Mission. Whether Ashley knew about the London City Mission or not in 1836 is uncertain; he certainly got to know about it soon after, and gave it the same hearty support. The L.C M. was started by a mission-minded Scotsman, David Nasmith, who settled in London early in 1835, having already established undenominational, layman-operated missions in Glasgow, Dublin and New York. Seeking patronage and funds, he soon found that he had come to a climate that made interdenominational co-operation very difficult. Bishop Blomfield received him kindly, but gave him no encouragement. He got valuable countenance and financial help from some eminent Evangelical laymen (Thomas Fowell Buxton was the one who mattered most) and some of the less eminent Evangelical clergy; but the regular use of lay agents, not to mention the application of partly Church of England funds to partly Nonconformist ends, so affrighted the Bishop of London, Blomfield, that in 1839 he positively ordered his clergy to resign from it. Edward Bickersteth no doubt endeared himself to Ashley by persisting – under, as his biographer said, 'circumstances which involved some self-denial and moral courage' – in preaching on its behalf.[1]

The L.C.M. prospered despite the frowns of ecclesiastical power, extended its operations throughout the metropolis, and diversified them so as to combine every kind of charitable relief and social rescue work with its proselytizing. Many of

1 T. R. Birks, *Memoir of Bickersteth* (1852), ii. 143.

the new metropolitan philanthropic groups that sprouted in the 1840s and 1850s seem to have at least part of their origin in the L.C.M.; and to it Ashley was largely indebted for his introduction to the London slums. The L.C.M.'s reliance upon lay missionaries and its ingenuous disregard of the claims of the historic Churches continued to keep many potential well-wishers away; but Ashley blamed them for being too fastidious. In his speech at the 1873 meeting of the C.P.A.S., when he really let himself go, he criticized them for having been too respectable, conventional and snobbish.

We are all beset and bound in the Church by starch and buckram, just as all departments of the Government are under the bondage of red tape. But . . . unless you can relax to a certain extent ceremony and ecclesiastical etiquette, so far as is not inconsistent with sound principle, you can never hope to reach even the fringes of the people whom you desire to recover.

How, he asked, had the light of religion been kept burning at all for tens of thousands of Londoners? – 'By a certain set of eccentric and abnormal teachers, good, kind, excellent men, but not called to do the work by any regular ordination, self-appointed, and engaged in that particular vocation simply from their own propensity that way, and a single desire to do good.'

Other parts of that speech were still more startling. He revealed himself as a Church reformer of the most radical kind; and his proposals amounted to a series of smacks in the face for the bishops. That Shaftesbury was unecclesiastical has by now been made sufficiently clear; it remains to show in what respects he was also anticlerical. 'I am not', he admitted on this celebrated occasion, 'such a lover of episcopacy as to think it necessary for salvation.' He would like to see the episcopate remodelled after the semi-presbyterian pattern proposed by Archbishops Ussher and Leighton 200 years or so before. He was sure that 'nothing would more tend to induce great numbers of people to join our Church than the putting an end to a state of things under which Ordination is left in the hands of a single individual'. After this, it could come as no surprise to learn that he was against any reform of the system of patronage that would give the bishops a larger share of it, and in favour of removing them from the House of Lords if the number of dioceses could not otherwise be doubled

To many, these must have appeared as the utterances of an angry, cranky old man. To some extent, they were. He was old, he was angry, and he was inclined to be cantankerous. But what he was saying was in no way inconsistent with the line of his thinking since the later 1830s. Of course he was wary of bishops, as any keen Protestant was bound to be, for the simple reason that Papists and Puseyites made much of them. But there was more to his dislike of episcopacy than that. Experience had quickly convinced him that the existing ecclesiastical set-up, with the bishops stiffly in control of it, did little to serve God in the ways that, by his reading of the signs of the times, mattered most: the spread of the Gospel in plain Evangelical terms, the subordination of national policies to God's laws, and the vigorous prosecution of social reform. He always kept a careful watch on the bishops' voting in the upper house. Again and again he had found them in his path. He had found less dignified clergymen in his path too; that would sadden or annoy him, but not overmuch, for he recognized no significant difference of quality or function between clergymen and laymen and never seriously expected the former to act differently from the latter. But bishops, whom he viewed simply as a species of superclergymen, invited a stricter judgment. What were they for, with all their pomp and pretensions, if not to set conspicuously good examples? And what was their use, if they showed no more zeal or activity for God's work on earth than all the laymen of comparable (not to mention lower!) social station who ran the societies and associations by which that work was, in the main, prosecuted?

Shaftesbury never had much patience with the dignitaries of the Church. When, for instance, the conservatives of the Church were seeking to rally opinion against Gladstone's Irish Church policy, he noted how stupidly their clericalism and snobbery had led them to set about it:

– in a moment of haste and rashness, the Archbishop of Canterbury was announced to preside over a grand gathering in St James's Hall! No preparation, no securing of good lay names, of merchants, bankers, lawyers etc. – And what was the issue? – An immense host of clergy and prelates, a few peers of little note, and a weak display to the world that a belief still remained that the public could be bebishoped and beduked into a submissive line of thought. [8 September 1868.]

Becoming a bishop, he thought, had a bad effect on men. Even a good Evangelical would assume new dignity with the office, and watch carefully lest his old Nonconformist friends should compromise him. Shaftesbury's part in securing the appointment of so many Evangelical bishops during Palmerston's premiership must not give the impression that he cared much about them. Better, indeed, that episcopal thrones should seat Evangelicals rather than the covert or open 'ritualists' whom Gladstone would propose if he got the chance; but few of these men whom Shaftesbury nominated were personal friends of his. Their theology was sound and safe and they could be relied on not to flirt with the Scarlet Woman; but by this time of his life Shaftesbury had long given up his early hopes that zeal for the service of God in practical, social, self-sacrificing ways would generally be found in company with correct Evangelical faith. Experience had taught him that the technically 'pious' could not be relied on for support, while the technically 'worldly' were often surprisingly helpful. In the same way, he had found that Nonconformists might be more helpful than Church people, and Shaftesbury insisted on judging by deeds as well as by professions of faith. 'Many Dissenters', he noted of the attendance at one of his early Ragged School meetings; 'but it is high time to be thinking where we agree, not where we differ' (27 November 1845). Criticized for hobnobbing with them, he boldly justified himself. 'I conceive I am acting in the spirit of the Bible and the spirit of the Church of England. . . . But, if the conduct I pursue be at variance with the doctrines and requirements of the Established Church, I shall prefer to renounce communion with the Church to abandoning these wretched infants [to] oppression, infidelity, and crime' (11 December 1845). Only one bishop ever publicly countenanced the Ragged Schools, and that was Edward Stanley of Norwich, a man so broad in his theological principles as to be reputed not much better than a Unitarian. In theory, Shaftesbury abhorred such men; but did not their practice show them better Christians than many who were more orthodox? So he was glad, though surprised, to see Stanley there, and was led to a characteristic reflection upon the strait-laced Blomfield: 'Why does not my Lord of London inspect, personally, the sinks and gutters of his own miserable diocese? Alas, though he have some zeal, he has more dignity' (19 March 1846). Blomfield stood branded as a bit of a humbug; and Shaftesbury, who hated humbug, was particularly severe when he thought he detected it in dignitaries of the Church. He was never severer than when, in 1847, the Dean and Chapter of Hereford, after making a fine fuss about the appointment of Oxford's supposedly unorthodox Professor Hampden to their see, knuckled under at the last moment and admitted him. 'The Dean,' he noted, 'having gallantly protested, sworn, imprecated, and prospectively embraced poverty and dishonour, made a grand speech and affixed the capitular seal, the token of unanimity. This was a clever way of saving his bacon! – keeping his engagement, and shirking his praemunire' (30 December 1847).

This remarkable anticlericalism, which lay never far below Shaftesbury's surface, was apt to erupt violently when joined by his more commonplace antisacerdotalism. Like so many ardent Protestants of his age, he easily became passionate about Popery, and especially when it seemed to be infiltrating the Established Church. Whether this fear of 'priestcraft' brought out the best or the worst in Shaftesbury, readers must judge for themselves. It certainly brought out some of the strongest sides of his character.

Roman Catholicism in itself did not greatly inflame him. He never liked it, of course; he thought it idolatrous, super- stitious, and despotic; but he had sense and virtue enough to see that with its baser parts many better ones were mingled, and he never visited a Papist country without remarking objectively on both. In the United Kingdom, Popery mattered mainly as part of the Irish question. Roman Catholics were indeed becoming more numerous in England and Scotland, with the influx of Irish labour and, in the higher ranks of society, a succession of conversions which both parties, for their own purposes, took equal pains to publicize; but still they remained socially insignificant and politically negligible. Shaftesbury never indulged in the vulgar sort of 'No Popery!' language that attracted many Evangelicals and gave religious demagogues like Hugh Stowell and Hugh McNeile (neither of whom attracted him) their popular following; indeed he agreed with Lord John Russell that such 'unmeasured violence' was wholly reprehensible (31 October 1846). He went temporarily berserk about Popery in 1850–1, but so did almost everyone else – including Lord John Russell. Popery in Ireland of course worried him more, because of the larger numbers involved, because of the equivocal status of Protestant establishment there, and because he understood how the Irish felt about it (see pages 73–4). But no more than British Popery did Irish make him intemperate or intolerant. In common with many other intelligent Protestants he voted for 'Catholic emancipation' in 1829 and, disappointed by its aftermath, later regretted it. He respected the liberty of the Irish – as of any people, for that matter – to worship as they liked. He thought it a pity they were Papists, not least because he believed their chances of improving their wordly condition were thereby diminished; he was inevitably a supporter of Protestant missionary work among them; but he was cautious and delicate about it, because the missionaries (especially when they were themselves Irish) were so often coarse and offensive. He believed that the British had in the past treated the Irish so badly that they had a duty to treat them generously. Yet his Protestant principles forbade him to countenance any actual assistance of Popery by the State. That would be not justifiable Christian charity, but inexcusable national apostasy. So in 1845 he came out strong in opposition when Peel proposed greatly to increase the government's annual grant to

Maynooth seminary, and so succeeded in his aim to 'avoid harsh or personal expressions' without compromising his Protestant principles that he won compliments from all parties. When Gladstone disestablished the Irish Church twenty years or so later, Shaftesbury preserved a remarkable calm, taking no strong part one way or the other. 'It is for England the most serious day since the Reformation,' he wrote. 'He may be opening the way to such a revival of Papal power as may make the most scoffing to tremble. He may be preparing such a career for the Protestant belief as may make the Roman Catholics curse the day in which he was born.' Shaftesbury, however, soon withdrew the credit he had been inclined to give Gladstone for so much boldness and lofty idealism. 'His dearest and most intimate friend the Duke of Argyll told my mother-in-law that "there was really no other way of getting Dizzy out of office!" Well, well, well, would not St Paul repeat in this day, "All seek their own, not the things that are Jesus Christ's"' (30 March 1868).

Thus Shaftesbury was far from immoderate when he faced Popery proper. It was a different matter when he was confronted with what he understood to be Popery in a dishonest Anglican disguise. In his rage and indignation he was not at all singular; the men of the Oxford Movement – Tractarians or 'Puseyites', as they were popularly known – and the Anglo-Catholics or 'ritualists' who soon took the movement to a very Popish-looking extremity, were apt to inflame the fury of any serious Protestant; and baiting or vilifying these supposed traitors became a common Protestant occupation and amusement at many levels beside that high theological one on which alone controversy could be conducted with some effect. Ashley operated, on the whole, on the lower levels. Intellectually, he was of course as capable of following the intricacies of the argument as any of the professional theologians involved; and it is fairly clear from some of his letters and meditations that he did so. But he conceived that his duty, as a public man, lay in the rousing and leadership of public opinion, a business demanding no great refinement of logic or learning; and in the bringing to bear of public pressure

wherever it could thwart the plotters. In any case, Tractarianism made him too angry for any higher role. It made him very
angry indeed, and provoked him to several of his most
extravagant acts.

His friend Lord Morpeth (who became seventh Earl of
Carlisle in 1848) began the popular Protestant hue and cry
against the Puseyites in the summer of 1838. In a widely
reported speech in the Commons he called attention to their
'romanizing' tendencies as revealed in the literary *Remains* of
Richard Hurrell Froude, a propaganda work recently published by Newman and Keble to keep fresh the memory of
their just-deceased young friend. Their management of the
opposition to Dr Hampden's appointment as Regius Professor of Divinity in 1836 had already drawn upon them some
suspicions of unscrupulousness and malignance; but the
Evangelicals had been as keen as the High Churchmen to do
Hampden down – it was only the first of a series of occasions
when the High and Low were to drop their bickering in
order to jump on the Broad – and it needed some special shock
to make the more Evangelical and Protestant parts of the
religious public realize what the men of Oxford were doing:
that they were not just continuing in a more spirited style the
old High Church campaigns against Erastianism, Calvinism
and Latitudinarianism, to all of which the Protestants were
well accustomed, but that they were actually presenting a
perfectly new and very menacing pistol at the Protestants'
heads. The publication of Froude's *Remains* woke the
Protestants up. Once awake, they looked at their earlier Tracts
more carefully, and found plenty to worry them; they watched
the Tractarians' doing like hawks, and caught them out again
and again.

It was at this stage of the affair that Ashley joined in, re-
vealing for the first time what he was often, unfortunately, to
reveal again: a talent for reckless and inaccurate denunciation.
This was not his inevitable habit. He could be cautious,
meticulous, moderate and charitable, and often was. But
sometimes he saw red, and then he apparently lost the use of
his scholarly faculties, and some of his Christian charity too.

The Puseyites acted on him in this way. About Pusey himself, Ashley's feelings were ambivalent. Pusey was his cousin (Ashley's father's mother was Pusey's aunt); they had been up at Christ Church together; Ashley loved him for his gentleness, his piety, his self-sacrificing munificence; and although for forty years he never relaxed hostility towards the Puseyites, Ashley never ceased to show peculiar tenderness towards their leader. Always looking out for the chance of a truce or an armistice, he reciprocated that inner yearning for reconciliation that Pusey clearly felt too. Each man appreciated the other's rare quality. Pusey died the first. 'Sept. 23rd. – My friend Pusey, dead and buried. Intensely and fearfully as I differed from him in many points of unspeakable importance, I could not but love the man.' Each loved the other despite his theology. Beyond his theology, however, one feels that Shaftesbury's conduct towards Pusey and Pusey's party required a good deal of forgiving. It was Ashley who took the lead in running a rival to the mild Isaac Williams for the poetry professorship in the winter of 1841-2. It was not he who first thought of contesting the election; but once the battle was on, he joyously joined in, and at once outpaced its originators. The rival candidates' merits as poets or critics of poetry soon became quite immaterial. They stood simply for or against the Tractarians. In his first letter published in *The Times*, on 11 December 1841, Ashley took this ground quite unashamedly. Under the circumstances such a ground was far from inexcusable. What was less excusable, however, was the way Ashley denounced Williams, almost certainly without having read him; certainly without having understood him, or taken any pains to do so. The Tractarian lawyer Roundell Palmer, who answered Ashley's letters, charitably inferred that 'Lord Ashley had been misled by someone not altogether worthy of his confidence'.[1] This was probably what

1 For this curious affair, see Roundell Palmer (Earl of Selborne), *Memorials: Family and Personal* (1896), i. 339–45; Liddon's *Life of Pusey*, ii. 260–7; and Hodder, i. 388–98. Ashley's state of mind (or that of his informant) appears in his describing Williams's tracts *On Reserve in Communicating Religious Knowledge* as his tract on 'Reserve in

happened. Ashley was easily led when his blood was up, easily 'stoked up' as Cavour once put it, easily egged on to displays of extravagance or petulance; as Gladstone gently remarked, 'he was liable to influence from an entourage inferior to himself'.[2] But he was far too tough a character to be led, far too intelligent and well educated to be taken in, except when he wanted to be so. The truth is, that Ashley's passions and prejudices were capable of bringing him down to a discreditable, vulgar level of thought and conduct; and that he rarely hit a lower level than when his Protestant passions and prejudices encountered Puseyism. Thus it was in this instance. Thus it was ten years later when, on the platform of the Bible Society at Exeter Hall, he said that Tractarianism was, 'of all the isms that ever existed . . . the most offensive and, in many respects, the most deceitful and hypocritical,' being actually in alliance with infidelity against Evangelicalism! Besides being rubbish, this was slanderous; but Shaftesbury was pleased with himself about it.[3] Thus it was, again and again.

Extreme and intemperate in attitude towards men who inclined to believe too much, he was the same towards those who declined to believe enough. When W. H. Brookfield (a highly intelligent schools inspector, theologically non-partisan) said in course of a sermon at Berkely Chapel that it was not absolutely necessary to salvation to believe that Christ was tempted in the wilderness by the conventional physical Devil, Shaftesbury rose, hat in hand, and walked out. He subsequently told Palmerston that Brookfield could not

Preaching the Doctrine of the Atonement', and in the amazing summary he gives of its contents.He ran through a similar series of misrepresentations in the violent attacks he made upon the Scottish Episcopal Church in late 1876. This affair may be studied in the several pamphlets that sustained it; it is not mentioned by Hodder.

[2]British Museum Additional Manuscripts, 44773/13. Hodder, iii. 123–4, seems to admit this.

[3]See his letter to Alexander Haldane, in Hodder, ii. 402. The speech is not mentioned. This is one of the many occasions when Hodder, evidently sensitive about them, draws a veil over Shaftesbury's least defensible episodes.

possibly be made a bishop – the man was a 'freethinker'![1]
That finished Brookfield! John Seeley's *Ecce Homo* he felt
moved to describe as the 'most pestilential book ever vomited
from the jaws of hell', Bishop Colenso's *Critical Examination
of the Pentateuch* as a 'puerile and ignorant attack on the
unassailable Word of God'. To John Stuart Mill he referred
at least once in his diary as 'Antichrist' (19 November 1868).
He lumped all liberal theologians together as 'Neologians'.
He did not try to ascertain exactly what their views were. He
knew enough about them if he knew that they doubted
the verbal inspiration of the Scriptures. It never entered his
head that he might be misrepresenting them, or that it mattered if he did, or that they might be seeking to spread the
saving truths of the Scriptures just as he was. This is a bit
odd, inasmuch as in some moods he seemed to be himself
aware of the intellectual difficulties presented by the traditional approach to the Bible, and to share the 'Neologians''
confidence that free inquiry could not hurt its essential
message. 'Try the Scriptures intellectually merely, and you will
encounter no end of difficulties', he once wrote. 'Try them by
the heart, and you will find such a flood of comfort, conviction and assurance, that all difficulties will vanish . . .' (31
January 1871). 'It is not the real knowledge, but the ignorance
of scientific men that does mischief' (29 August 1863). With
reflections such as these, he would have had the glad agree-
ment of every thinking theologian who was anxiously striving
to keep Christianity credible for the intellectually more active
and advanced sections of the population as well as for the
simple and ignorant. But such lucid intervals were not
common, and hardly ever showed in public; and their force
was in any case far weaker than that of the literalist convictions and compulsive emotions that kept his mind closed on all
theological and religious questions.

His mind was so closed, in fact, that as he got older he found
himself increasingly isolated. What 'Evangelicalism' implied,
he no longer understood. Obviously the party was losing, from
the sixties onwards, whatever unity of mind and will it had

1 C. and F. Brookfield, *Mrs Brookfield and her Circle* (1905), ii, 441.

earlier possessed. Perhaps there never was an Evangelical *party* worth speaking of during Victoria's reign. In the early years of the century, when Wilberforce and other great men of Clapham had provided a recognizable sort of directorate for the movement, it was fairly clear who they were and what they stood for. But no comparably homogeneous group of leaders took their place when they deceased, as most of them did just about the time that Shaftesbury was becoming involved in the movement; and besides, their very success in diffusing Evangelical standards, sentiment and manners, helped to make continued coherence more and more difficult. There was so much Evangelicalism of one kind and another about in early Victorian Britain, that the historian cannot define it further than by noting what, in general, men who were ready to acknowledge themselves as Evangelicals believed, and by noticing how similar their reactions were to certain stimuli – Popery, Puseyism, Lord's Day Observance, liberal theology, slavery, overseas missions, dancing and the theatre, for example. But even on these especial interests of theirs, there was room for some diversity of opinion and emphasis; and on an ever larger number of great political, social and intellectual questions, they shared no common views at all. To speak of an 'Evangelical party' in the sixties is thus not very helpful, and is certainly much less meaningful than to speak of one in the tens or twenties.

Shaftesbury felt and deplored this growing loss of solidarity. He soon got sadly used to it in respect of his social questions – ' "sinners" were with me, "saints" against me', as he once put it (23 June 1842); but that men who claimed to be Evangelicals should not agree about religion, or about the most basic (as it seemed to him) applications of religion to politics – this he never understood; and it was on this account that he more and more defiantly classed himself as 'an Evangelical of the Evangelicals', a lonely faithful remnant. Other Evangelicals must, for their part, have found his rugged individuality puzzling as well as impressive, for he was not always as Evangelical as some Evangelicals thought they ought to be. He rebuffed an invitation in 1861 to head a society for 'the Evangelisation of Italy,' for he never waxed as ferocious against Popery *per se* as most of his Evangelical friends. His dislike of ecclesiasticism made his attitude towards establishment different from many of theirs. Many Evangelical churchmen gave much time to fighting Dissent. This seemed to Shaftesbury time wasted or misused; he had no sympathy with it. These were questions of 'applied theology'; but on more strictly theological questions, the same difference increasingly showed. Shaftesbury found himself out of sympathy with everybody during the agitation against Frederick Temples' elevation to the see of Exeter: 'a priest of Eleusis to the episcopal chair' was how he described it (8 October 1869). But how did his Evangelical friends take it? Some only opposed it out of hatred for Gladstone, the prime minster responsible. Some would not oppose it because it would set them on the same side as Pusey. Some spoke of Temple with unecessary violence; and some actually thought the appointment a good one.

They prefer . . . a Latitudinarian who would let them alone to a strict High Churchman who would be always intermeddling; that is, they prefer a Free Thinker who rejects the Atonement and the inspiration of Scripture, but who would be an ecclesiastical Gallio, to a bigot, who holds both, but in a meddling and authoritarian spirit. [23 October 1869]. Burgess, even Burgess, spoke to me . . . of Temple's 'delightful, Christian-like sermons'! [6 November 1869]. Miss Marsh, too, the daughter of that grand old Doctor, and herself an excellent, pious woman, writes to ask me, 'Why do you set on foot a "Crusade" against Dr Temple?' [9 November 1869].

There is no mistaking Shaftesbury's anger on this occasion; nor can one escape the conclusion that he was confused by it, as he found himself forced into a self-dramatized self-pitying isolation which would have been deplorable were it not much more pathetic.

If his claim to be an Evangelical of the Evangelicals rested, as he got older, on his retaining as beliefs what many of the more intelligent of them were discarding as superstitions, it rested in his earlier years on the adoption of certain beliefs to which only the more extreme of them adhered. This showed

most conspicuously in his beliefs about the Second Coming
of Christ and the Conversion and Restoration of the Jews –
matters which more moderate and cautious Evangelicals preferred to play down. About the Second Advent his beliefs were
not, indeed, as extreme as they might have been. He seems not
to have personally engaged in those brain-twisting calculations
of the date of the Second Coming, which, along with other
minute investigations of the prophecies, filled several specialist
'millenarian' periodicals and innumerable books and pamphlets through the middle decades of the century. No doubt
he recognized that the 'delicacy and difficulty of the subject'
was as great as in respect of 'Special Providences' (7 November 1848). But just as he nevertheless firmly believed in special
providences, so did he firmly believe that the Lord would
come, and not be slow. 'Every hour of reading, every hour of
reflection, strengthens me more and more, God be praised,
in the conviction that the Second Advent is the hope for all
the ends of the earth' (26 December 1847).

With the Second Advent was intimately connected the
promised Conversion and Restoration of the Jews, the ultra-
Evangelical topic that absorbed Ashley's religious energies
immediately after his conversion, and only slowly ceased to
obsess him. Evangelical prophetical exegetists could not
agree whether the Second Coming was to accompany, immediately to precede, or to follow the salvation of Israel. They
did agree that at any rate the two events would be closely
connected, as would be the conversion of the Jews and their
ingathering from their dispersion, to live again in their ancient
home.[1] It followed therefore that in working for either the
Jews' conversion or their reinstatement in the Holy Land,
Christians would infallibly bring nearer the glorious consum-
mation of all things, the final triumph of God. It appeared as
a way, if one may so describe it, of forcing God's hand,
hastening a process that might otherwise take longer; it gave
Evangelicals of the extremer sort great joy – 'a blessed subject,
and most comfortable', as Ashley put it (12 December 1848).

1 See Edward Bickersteth, *Practical Guide to the Prophecies* (7th ed.,
1845), esp. pp. 112–29.

'The conversion and salvation, the restoration and glory of Israel, will eminently display the glory of the triune Jehovah', wrote Edward Bickersteth, one of the leading exponents of this school.

What riches of forbearance, patience, long-suffering and faithfulness will it manifest in our heavenly Father! How wonderful the glories of his electing love in once rebellious and then recovered Israel! What efficacy in our Redeemer's blood! What a prevalency in his intercession for his worst and bitterest enemies! . . . Oh what a bright and valuable jewel in the Redeemer's *many* crowns (Rev. xxix. 12) at the latter day, will be converted Israel, holy and joyful in their own land![1]

Ashley enthusiastically threw himself into this side of Evangelicism. He patronized the 'Jews' Society' (as the London Society for Promoting Christianity among the Jews was generally known) and took conscientious delight in paying his respects to such Jews as he ever came near. At Carlsbad he perhaps slightly astonished the other aristocratic visitors when, noticing 'many Jews here in their costumes', he 'bowed to several, to show my respect for the nation. I shall next open a conversation with some of them' (14 August 1843). The only thing that kept him from absolutely detesting Disraeli was Disraeli's brave and constant advocacy of Jewish claims; and although he did not agree with Dizzy that they should be admitted to full civil equality with Christians, he spoke of them much more warmly than many who did, saying on one occasion:

He was not ashamed to confess that he regarded the very poorest Israelite with feelings akin to reverence, as one of the descendants of the most remarkable nation that had ever yet appeared on the face of the earth – one of the forefathers of those who were yet to play the noblest part in the history of mankind.[2]

Ashley's special contribution to this Jewish cause was his support of the scheme for a Protestant bishopric in Jerusalem. This scheme, which presented diverse attractions to several classes of supporters, was first mooted by a Prussian states-

1 *Op. cit.*, P. 129.
2 16 December 1847. *Hansard*, 3rd series, xcv. 1272–82.

man, Bunsen, an active, forceful and persuasive Lutheran with
a lively interest in theology, a consuming passion for participation in ecclesiastical affairs, and considerable influence with
his pious sovereign, whom he persuaded to take up the idea
of a joint Anglo-Prussian, Lutheran-Anglican bishopric in
Jerusalem, partly to proselytize the Jews (a task lamentably
neglected by the Christian churches already established there),
partly to stand for Protestant interests and principles in a
place where Roman Catholics and Eastern Orthodox unfairly
dominated what was a common Christian concern, and partly
also an oblique contribution towards the strengthening of
Prussian and, more obviously, British political power in the
Levant. Between his first becoming aware of it (8 October
1838), and its accomplishment three years later, Ashley worked
diligently to publicize the project and to badger his aristocratic
friends and acquaintances in the government to give it their
support. One may doubt whether any of them took his religious
arguments seriously. Palmerston, who was Foreign Secretary
for most of this time, was of all men most unlikely to do so.
Ashley sadly noted that 'he weeps not like his Master over
Jerusalem, nor prays that now, at last, she may put on her
beautiful garments'. But Ashley's other arguments, political,
financial and commercial, struck home. Pam saw his way to
incorporating the idea in his grand designs for a settlement of
the Turkish question, and thus gave Ashley the first of many
causes to bless him. The general public showed some enthusiasm, seeing the scheme rather imprecisely as a sort of
crusade and a snub to the Russians and the French. Only some
of the Puseyites persisted in throwing cold water on it; for
which Ashley was not inclined to love them the more. The
change of administrations, from Melbourne's to Peel's, at a
critical stage of the negotiations, made Ashley's services as an
arranger of meetings and smoother of paths all the more
valuable. Anticipating difficulties from Pam's successor Lord
Aberdeen, Ashley wrought incessantly with the new prime
minister, and won his rather cold and puzzled support. The
Act settling the terms of British participation passed on
22 September; Moses Solomon Alexander was consecrated on

7 November; and when he set off for Palestine a few days later, with an entourage of missionaries, children, and a pregnant wife that astonished Roman Catholic witnesses of his progress, it was in the 'Admiralty steamboat' which Ashley had earnestly begged Peel to make available. 'Had I not been almost accustomed, so to speak, to God's mercies,' noted Ashley, ' I should have disbelieved it. . . . "Surely the Isles shall wait for thee and the ships of Tarshish first, to bring thy sons from afar and thy daughters from the ends of the earth" ' (25 October 1841).

This peculiar missionary bishopric, the product of such mixed motives, the vehicle of such unrealistic aspirations, never did much good; its unhealthy life was allowed to expire with the decease of its then occupant in 1881, and when it was reconstituted it was in a more regular Anglican style. Newman's verdict on it, that he never heard of any good or any harm that it had done, is well known; and although Newman's judgment might be suspected as that of a partisan, it is difficult to fault him here. Few Jews were ever converted – very few, considering the amount of money being spent; and it was reasonably supposed by the institution's critics, who only became more numerous as time went by, that the material advantages seen to accompany conversion might have had a lot to do with what conversions there were. Some of the missionaries under the bishop's tenuous care showed as much interest in 'converting' Roman Catholic and Orthodox Christians as in the Jews. To the evidences of enthusiasm and gullibility which marked many of the Jews' Society's doings was soon added a strong suspicion that they were covering up a series of scandals alleged against Bishop Alexander's even more enthusiastic successor Samuel Gobat. His accusers, an ostensibly trustworthy group including two Scottish doctors, Alexander M'Caul himself, and the painter William Holman Hunt found the Committee of the Jews' Society impervious to their demands for a judicial inquiry. They were stonewalled by Bishop Villiers and by Shaftesbury, who at the 1857 general meeting publicly deprecated any further discussion of the matter, and in his preface of the 'Official Life' of Gobat

blandly passed over it.[1] It is almost impossible to believe that
Gobat's accusers were mistaken, quite impossible to believe
that Shaftesbury and his colleagues in the Jews' Society behaved properly.[2]

Shaftesbury comes out of the story badly. Having once
taken up religious cudgels on someone's behalf (as he had
done before Gobat's consecration, when the man's suitability
was publicly questioned), he did not like subsequently to
admit that he might have been wrong. That fickle readiness
to suspect the worst, those rapid alternations of judgment,
which marked his attitudes towards so many people, were
easily anaesthetized whenever he was Evangelically committed; he became disarmed of the ordinarily critical faculties
which, had they only been awake, would have protected him
from much disappointment and humiliation. The Gobat
affair was an illustration of this, as was the story of the
Malta Protestant College, of which Gobat was for a while
Vice-Principal.[3] An even more signal one was when one of the
senior staff of the London Reformatory was discovered to
have been taking sexual advantage of his position there for
years. Shaftesbury was properly horrified and distressed; but
the terms in which he confided his distress to his diary make
even a sympathetic reader wonder whether he had not brought
it on himself.

The thing that troubles me the most [he wrote] is the mysteriousness
of God's providence. For six years a body of pious, praying Christian men, not pursuing philanthropy from mere sentiment or natural
feelings, as Unitarians might do, but in the depths and fervour of
Evangelical life, have been suffered to go on in blindness, ignorance
and delusion. . . . If there has been one thing which, for years and
years, I have prayed more than another, it is comprized in these

1 *Life and Work of Samuel Gobat* (1884).

2 My account of this affair is based mainly on *The Christian Remem-
brancer*, July 1858, xxxvi. 171–237, and Samuel McCau, *Jerusalem: the
Bishop, its Missionaries and its Converts* (1866). The several biographies
of Gobat are historically worthless.

3 See Hodder, iii. 179–81. *The Record*, 16 and 23 March 1846 and 2
April 1846 chronicles its early stages. 'Fr. Achilli' was later, one is not
surprised to learn, one of its staff.

sentences, 'Commit thy ways unto the Lord, and He will direct thy paths. . . .' 'In thee have I trusted, let me never be confounded.' I am, I fear, confounded; never can I hope to think or speak with confidence again. . . . It is utter and irrecoverable loss of character, and, in that, of usefulness. [25 May 1855.]

Within a few days, however, he was the same old Shaftesbury again, confident and useful as ever. It never occurred to him that he might have done well to pray less and think more.

To those who know Shaftesbury solely as the great philanthropist and/or the great Evangelical, it may come as something of a surprise to learn that he was always keenly interested in foreign and imperial affairs. While he lived, indeed, this interest of his was taken for granted, and men looked confidently to him for pungent contributions to most of the big debates. Since his death, this side of him has been more and more forgotten, and not unreasonably so, inasmuch as he left no mark on the imperial and foreign affairs of Britain comparable to that which he made on the religious and social. The latter suffice to show his quality and greatness. Yet the former demand at any rate a few pages, partly because some of his deepest beliefs about men and society showed most clearly only when he was looking at other societies from without, and partly because as a religious man he viewed international politics, equally with domestic, as a matter for conscientious judgment, and was aware of no difference between them as scenes of the workings of God's providence.

Shaftesbury was a great believer in freedom, and was prepared to go a good way further than most Conservative Victorian statesmen to spread and secure it. His Conservatism, as to which he was always emphatic, was singular in this respect as in every other. He looked as eagerly as any self-styled Liberal for signs that Britain's peculiar blessing of 'civil and religious liberty' was taking root or flourishing elsewhere. Of course, he was not generally as optimistic and unguarded as Liberals were apt to be about its chances – except when he thought he saw prophecies of the fall of Rome being fulfilled. (For example, 18 June 1848: 'Marvellous,

marvellous accounts from Rome! . . . Are not all the powers
preparing to "eat her flesh, and burn her with fire"?') He had
no illusions about the unpreparedness of most populations for
self-government. Cherishing the aristocratic principle as highly
as he did, and loathing the unconsidered shedding of blood,
he could not associate comfortably with a movement so largely
democratic and revolutionary. Yet neither could he permanently and uncritically oppose it. He was no democrat,
but he was perhaps a little of a demagogue; and one can certainly imagine Shaftesbury participating in a revolution, had
he been born in Milan, say, or Budapest, instead of in Grosvenor Square.

There was more explosive material in Lord Shaftesbury
than he was always aware of; and there was at the same time
more delicate perceptiveness and more sound sense when it
came to general political questions than you would expect to
find in a self-styled Conservative aristocrat with a penchant
for proclaiming doom and decline. For example, he never
forgot the supreme importance of public opinion. Much
of his life's work was devoted to raising its tone and to
bringing its force to the support of his causes. Politicians and
pressure-groupers who thought they could defy or do without
it seemed to him simply inept. In contemplating the great
urban masses of population, he often reflected that nothing
but what he most commonly called 'sentiment' restrained them
from anarchy and violence. It was the same highly intelligent
appreciation of the power of ideas that led him to one of his
boldest displays of political independence: his leading the
attack, in the Lords, on Victoria's proposed new title of Empress. He may have been mistaken in his intuition that the
British public would take less kindly to the rule of an Empress
than to that of a Queen; but he put his finger on the central
fact of liberal constitutionalism when he warned the peers
and Dizzy's Faery Queen: 'Now that the principle of Divine
right to the Throne has departed from the people – now that
they are in possession of almost universal suffrage – your
Lordships' House and the Throne itself are upheld by senti-

ment alone, and not by force or superstition. Loyalty is a sentiment. . . .'[1]

Shaftesbury loved the classical virtues of patriotism, loyalty and public service, and knew they could not flourish without close kinship of feeling between rulers and ruled. An ignorant and stubborn ruler (such as he believed Victoria to be) was liable to chill them. Under an alien or despotic ruler, they could hardly live at all, to the great impoverishment of the community. His anxiety on this score, coupled with his delicate historical sense, underlay that remarkable sensitivity he often showed towards national feelings, habits and prejudices, as well as sympathetic respect for the national principle. Thus his tenderness towards the Irish, 'that wronged and insulted people – wronged, I mean, by our ancestors' (24 June 1869); his moving reflections on the condition of the Italians, cited above (page 34), his forgiving much pagan folly in 'the bigoted, ignorant Papist who sits on the throne of Bavaria' on account of the admirable effort he was making 'in favour of German nationality' (6 October 1843); his sympathy 'with the Scottish people in their resistance to English aggressions' (26 August 1839). His hatred of despotism, Roman, Austrian or Russian, rested partly on his belief that its self-protective and expansive tendencies alike could only operate to the detriment of legitimate national interests. It was not the physical power of despotism that in itself repelled him, but the principles which necessarily governed its use.

Himself, he was not afraid of power, for he believed he would make moral use of it, to promote the greater glory of God. Nor was he more than cautious about the extension of British imperial power, for that seemed to him capable of similar beneficent use. A nation blessed by God with freedom, wealth and true religion was under the same obligation as a comparably fortunate individual to spread its blessings far and wide. Shaftesbury envisaged Britain's role in Europe as one of moral influence and example; he was particularly hurt when the calamities of the Crimean War made Britain

1. 3 April 1876. *Hansard*, 3rd series.

ridiculous, and wrote to Evelyn: 'We hear the words of Isaiah, "Come and sit down in the dust." Constitutional government is a laughing-stock, and the progress of rational freedom on the Continent is checked for half a century.' A few years later he played a very conspicuous part in whipping up public support for the cause of Italian independence. The prospect of religious liberty and the Bible freely circulating in Italy (prospects which Cavour and his agents in Britain took pains to impress on Shaftesbury!) were like petrol poured on the always smouldering embers of his sympathy for nationalist and constitutionalist movements. He flared up into several very declamatory public statements, the richest of which made Palmerston's and Earl Russell's essays in the same genre seem quite pale by comparison; and to begin with he praised the noble and disinterested conduct of Napoleon III in terms which made his calmer friends smile or sigh. His conduct, as usual, was impetuous; but his principles were beyond criticism. 'I protest', he said when opposing the French annexation of Savoy, 'against the policy of treating nations like flocks of sheep. . . . We in this country have long protested against the traffic in human flesh; I equally protest against any traffic in human or national rights.'[1] He spoke even more vigorously on behalf of the Poles when they rebelled against the Russians in 1863.

The same burning desire for righteousness and justice in the conduct of international affairs led him, in 1843, to lodge a noble protest against British participation in the opium trade, and a year later to bring a formidable indictment against Peel's government for its insolent and despotic treatment of the Ameers of Scind. Into the merits of that case it is not necessary to go further than to note that Peel and his cabinet colleagues, amongst themselves, shared the steadily growing public belief that Lord Ellenborough, their Governor-General, had in fact dealt rather unjustly with those defeated Indian rulers. Only severe administrative difficulties and the politician's perennial necessity to save face prevented them from

1. 7 February 1860. *Hansard*, 3rd series, clvi. 594–5.

acknowledging it publicly. Shaftesbury, as we have already seen and shall shortly see again, was himself no paragon when it came to admitting having been in the wrong; and it might be debated to the end of time whether a Tory prime minister who knew he was in the wrong but would not publicly admit it was really more culpable than a very influential and high-minded independent Tory who, sometimes in the wrong himself, was sometimes incapable of realizing it. That, however, is a different question from the purely political one in which Ashley was here figuring. No believer in representative and responsible government can doubt that one of the most valuable services a representative can perform is to indict dubious acts of government on the highest and most formidable grounds going. Ashley's Toryism never prevented him from doing this, even when the Tories were in power (indeed, he did it the more zestfully when Peel was in power, because he thought Peel's motives were always so low); and he did this sort of thing supremely well. In the peroration of his magnificent speech he touched on several of his imperial *idées fixes.*

Sir [he said] we are often admonished, with oracular solemnity, that our empire in Hindustan is founded on opinion. Is it the opinion of our justice, our humanity, or our power? A wise and patriotic Government would ardently pursue such a noble combination. Sir, the generosity of absolute power is cheap and safe and honourable; true principle alone is of so attractive a nature as to lead many to believe that a really Christian empire would soon acquire the sovereignty of the world by the voluntary and eager resort of all nations under the shadow of its wings. Whether, by such means as these, Great Britain shall accomplish the dominion of the East, remains to be seen. We have not, I fear, made an auspicious beginning; but if we are to gain no more by virtue, let us not lose what we have by injustice. . . .

For thus maintaining the cause of 'heathens' against 'Christians', Ashley incurred much criticism from fellow Evangelicals. *The Record* newspaper, not quite yet under the control of his friend Alexander Haldane, was 'as usual . . . very offensive. . . . "The champion of profligate men"! " The reverse of Wilberforce"! and such like . . .' (13 February 1844). He heard that Bishop Sumner of Chester had been parroting this party line.

What a thing! 1. If these people [the Ameers] are good enough for us to contract treaties with, they are good enough to enjoy the observance of them. 2. If we accept benefits from those people, we must also repay them. 3. A Christian kingdom may refuse all intercourse with its neighbours, but if it open an intercourse and derive advantages, it cannot turn round when well satiated and exclaim, 'By-the-by, a thought strikes me, you are so abominably wicked that really I must exterminate you!' 4. The principle of *The Record* and such would compel us to declare war against every Prince in Asia that kept more wives than one, would justify the Americans in repudiation, *et hoc genus omne*. [15 February 1844.]

Not all of his dealings with Indian questions were as excellent as this. His intellect did not always thus keep pace with his passions; and when his passions took control, he showed to less advantage. Thus was it with the Indian Mutiny. He seems never to have realized how ill he conducted himself in respect of the Mutiny, and if Edwin Hodder realized it he kept it to himself, for from his pages you would not gather half the truth.

The Indian Mutiny staggered the British public. It was so unexpected, so unaccountable. Its origins and character are still, after years of research by increasingly objective historians, not wholly clear. Small wonder, then, that as news of its outbreak and progress trickled home, rumour and surmise abounded. Inflamed by imperial egotism and hurt pride, the public was ready to believe the worst of the mutineers; and pretexts for doing so were quickly supplied by the more excited Britons in India, whose letters to private correspondents and newspaper editors alike handed on atrocity stories that lost nothing in the telling. There was some deliberate malignance in this, for the British community in Calcutta quickly lost confidence in the scrupulous and even-tempered Governor-General, Earl Canning, and by painting him as dilatory and feeble sought to have him recalled or put under pressure from home; but most of it was simply the fruit of fear, credulity and hysteria, and fairly obviously so, even then, to educated and dispassionate men with an ordinary know-ledge of the world.

Under the circumstances, it behoved responsible leaders of public opinion to withhold judgment until all the facts were known, and to refrain from exacerbating still further a public mind already sufficiently wild and dangerous. Shaftes-bury, however, made himself conspicuous as the chief encourager of popular frenzy. He swallowed all the tales he heard, and retailed them exuberantly. No other peer, no other individual of comparable standing, behaved as wildly; but then, none was at all like Shaftesbury. None was compounded of the same inflammable materials. Zeal for British imperial greatness, and belief in God's wish for it; unusually quick response to the suffering of women and children; conscientious delight in crusade-like causes, and joy in heading them; self-righteous impermeability to criticism, once he had staked his faith in such a cause; as extreme a tendency to believe the worst of men he considered 'bad' as to believe the best of the 'good', without attending to evidence in either case; some psychological instability and recklessness; and, most im-portant of all, the Evangelical's long-smouldering resentment at the government's fifty-year refusal to *establish* Protestant Christianity in India and actively to promote it: these elements of his mind and character now caught fire and set up a blaze that astonished all who beheld it. A passage from a letter written to Evelyn very early on (long before it was possible to know all the facts) will sufficiently indicate its quality.

The intelligence from India, though it fills me with horror, gives me no alarm. Could I set aside, forget, or cancel the unspeakable atrocities perpetrated on the women and children, I should rejoice in the event. We have acquired a power and a *right*, by the mutiny of these Sepoys, that we should never have attained had they con-tinued loyal, and a means of effecting reforms that, in other circum-stances, would either have been impossible, or have cost us years of delay. This outbreak presents a new picture in the history of man-kind – you may find abundant precedents for the *massacre* of women and children, but you will find none for the deliberate

sensual, gloating satisfaction of these fiends incarnate in the pro-
longed and refined suffering of babies. Day and night I think of
these things – what a worse than devil is man unsoftened by Christianity and left to himself! But the conduct of the British, collectively
and individually, in this awful crisis, has been supernatural. Everyone, male, female, infant, civilian, soldier, has exhibited an amount
of coolness, judgment, patriotism and intrepidity that fills me with
wonder; heartily do I bless God that He has so strengthened and
supported our people in this just cause.

During the autumn and winter of 1857 he made several big
speeches in this style. The one which attracted the most
attention, and subsequently got him into the most trouble, was
at Wimborne on 30 October. In the course of it he said:
'I myself saw a letter from the highest lady now in India
stating that day by day ladies were coming into Calcutta with
their ears and their noses cut off and their eyes put out.'
Other parts were still more horrific (for example, 'children
tortured in cold blood . . . before the eyes of their parents . . .
who were made to swallow portions of the flesh cut from the
limbs of the children, and themselves afterwards burnt over a
slow fire'), but this sentence caught the public eye, as clearly
referring to Lady Canning; and it was not forgotten by those
who, from a disinterested love of truth, a sympathetic understanding of India, or mere dislike of Shaftesbury, set about
checking his references. The showdown started at the end
of January 1858, when letters began to appear in *The Times*,
first to deny that the horrible and brutal murders in India
had been accompanied by such atrocious circumstances and
then denying, from personal knowledge, that Lady Canning
had ever written any such letter.[1] Nor, in fact, had she. News
of his speech had reached her by Christmas Eve, when,
writing home to Lord Granville, she remarked: 'Truth is not a
flourishing plant anywhere just at present. "The highest lady in
India" feels much inclined to call out Lord Shaftesbury.
What *can* he have said he *saw* in her letter? I certainly *heard*

1 *The Times*, 29 January, 2 and 3 February. That the greater part of the
atrocity stories were indeed untrue was soon demonstrated by Edward
Leckey, *Fictions connected with the Indian Outbreak of 1857* (Bombay,
1859).

of one lady without nose and ears, but never *believed* in her existence. . . .'[1] 'Shaftesbury could afford to ignore commonplace critics who signed themselves 'Vindex' and 'Lover of Accuracy' and was soon to show that he could insolently brush aside such plebeian (though not less accurate!) critics as plain Mr Hargreaves of Craven Hill Gardens;[2] but a slur on a peeress was a different matter. In a letter to *The Times* on 4 February he admitted that he should have said he had 'heard of' such a letter, and further implied that he knew he had been embroidering the truth about the massacres. A few days later Lord Granville wrote to Canning: 'Shaftesbury has been obliged to eat dirt about Lady Canning's letter, and is much abused for his inaccuracy and thirst for feeding the popular delusion whatever it may be.'[3] But that was not the end of Lady Canning's grievance. About the time Granville was writing to her husband, she got news of another of Shaftesbury's speeches, an 'abominably untrue one at Exeter Hall. I wish', she said, 'he would learn that it is wrong not to ascertain the truth of what he asserts.'[4]

Shaftesbury was unable to understand Lady Canning's point. He apologized for having unwarrantably referred to her (and indeed he had corrected the published reports of that speech as soon as he saw them), but it appears not to have entered his head that his real offence lay in having irresponsibly retailed rumours, inflamed passions, and hardened prejudices. In this affair, as in all affairs like it, he lost all the consistency, self-control and self-awareness that marked his conduct in other connexions; and none who knew him well were surprised when in the spring of 1858 he changed his tune and, after having made Canning's difficulties even greater than they need have been, suddenly appeared as one of the Governor-General's principal defenders.[5] Canning had shown that he

1 Lord Edmond Fitzmaurice, *Life of Earl Granville* (1905), i. 284.
2 See the *Saturday Review*, 27 March 1858.
3 Fitzmaurice, *op. cit.*, i. 289.
4 See A. J. C. Hare, *Two Noble Lives* (1893), ii. 422–3.
5 'Shaftesbury goes raving about the town,' reported Granville. 'He is much more violent for you than he was against you. He entirely forgets what he did in the autumn.' Fitzmaurice, *op. cit.*, i. 306.

was not all clemency by proclaiming confiscated the estates of those Indians in Oude (the seat of the revolt) who had not stayed loyal to the British Government. This measure was rather inconsiderately condemned by the new President of the Board of Control, Lord Ellenborough, in a peremptory despatch which was at once made the occasion of a full-scale attack on Derby's administration. Shaftesbury, who besides approving the confiscation of as much disloyal Indians' property as possible had long cherished a particular hatred of Lord Ellenborough, led the attack in the upper house with a sizzling speech in the grand manner. Lady Canning thanked him for it in a letter of remarkable tact and gentleness.[1] Once again Shaftesbury's faults had been forgiven by someone with plenty of cause to resent them.

1 Hodder, iii. 62, where it is presented as a reply to Shaftesbury's apology for his Wimborne speech. Unable to believe that Hodder was deliberately fibbing, I can only conclude that he shared Shaftesbury's hopeless confusion of mind about these Mutiny matters.

4

SATANIC MILLOWNERS, AND
SOME OTHERS

LORD SHAFTESBURY spent a large part of his life rescuing poor people from two sets of circumstances over which they had little or no control: bad employers and bad living conditions. For many poor people, of course, these circumstances coincided. Their employers were bad, and the conditions they lived in were bad. If they had no employers at all – if they were 'submerged' or 'sunk' (to use contemporary words for it) among the masses who were at best only casually employed – their living conditions might be so bad as to merit description as dying conditions. Shaftesbury knew all this. No other nobleman knew nearly as much about it. Few other men can have known much more. Shaftesbury became, during the eighteen-forties, one of the nation's experts on destitution. In Parliament he was looked to for authoritative speeches on it, and what he had to say was in the main exceedingly well worth listening to. His only faults, in this connexion, were his tendencies to credulity and exaggeration, which led him now and then to make bad or unusual aspects of the general question sound even worse or more bizarre than they actually were.[1] But these little failings kicked the beam when weighed against the breadth and depth of his knowledge, the good sense and practicality of his proposals, the unswerving devotion with which he pursued the question, the force and courage with which he compelled his often unwilling auditors to face up to it. And whatever exaggerations might be made, by Shaftesbury

[1] For example, his over-estimation of the number of mothers of young children working full-time in the cotton mills (see Margaret Hewitt, *Wives and Mothers in Victorian Industry* (1958)), and his swallowing a 'penitent convict's' account of the underworld's way of dealing with stolen plate that would not have been out of place in a G. W. M. Reynolds novel (see James Greenwood, *The Seven Curses of London* (1869), pp. 110–14).

or by anybody else, of particular aspects of destitution, of the extent and direness of that destitution in general there could be no exaggeration. Not until after Shaftesbury's death was its full extent charted and measured; not until the early years of our own century did institutions of voluntary social service and administrative organs of government, taken together, begin to become adequate to its handling. Shaftesbury only showed his singular mixture of sense, courage and perseverance year in year out, by harping on this theme throughout the second half of his long life.

He was concerned with poverty and destitution in all its forms, from all its causes; and, as we shall see in the next chapter, he was especially concerned with it in London, where were concentrated and displayed at their worst all its modern, urban causes and effects. His activities in this field – education, welfare, housing, health, missions, mere human rescue and salvage work – were of the highest value and importance, and would on their own have marked Shaftesbury as a great and good man. But they were not his first endeavours on behalf of the poor. These began much earlier, in 1833; they had reference not to the London poor but to those – not always quite so poor – of the new manufacturing districts in the Midlands and the North; and they must be treated as a separate group of activities, because his motives in engaging in them were, to begin with at any rate, quite different.

Ashley took up 'the factory question' as much from dislike of the millowners as from sympathy with the mill-workers. This fact (still often unrecognized) became obscured, during his own lifetime, by the development of his philanthropic activities. Six or seven years' experience of this question enlarged his mind to embrace the whole field of work for wages whether in textile mills or other types of factory, mines or brickfields, whether industrial or agricultural; that peculiar hatred of a special class of employer which first brought his attention to the problems of the wage-earner gradually dissolved, as the 1840s wore on, into a more general concern with all conditions of employment; that general commitment to all classes of employee in a special industry, gave away to a

special concern for women and children. His views changed
as his view widened, until by the 1860s it was as impossible to
distinguish between his concerns for different classes of the
poor as it would be pointless now to try to do so. But to begin
with, everything was sharper and more specific; and if the
nature of the impulse that originally involved him in the factory
question is not clearly understood, two consequences follow:
first, an important part of his social and political philosophy
lacks its brightest illustration, and second, the speed with
which he plunged into the question must make him seem even
more tempestuous than he actually was.

His involvement was sudden indeed. Before the autumn
of 1832 he knew very little about the factories. He did not even
know that a Select Committee of the Commons had been
taking evidence from their victims between April and August.
Only when that Committee's report came out, and filtered
into the newspapers, did he began to take an interest. He was,
he says in an autobiographical fragment written a few years
later, 'astonished and disgusted' by the stories of cruelty,
crippling, overwork, underpay, disease and death that then
widely circulated; and he wrote to Michael Sadler, the M.P.
hitherto in charge of the question who had just lost his seat
at the general election, to offer to present petitions (the staple
means by which popular movements then made themselves
felt in Parliament) or help in any other way he could. Nothing
immediately came of this, and Ashley says he had forgotten
the subject when, early in February 1833, his Tory colleague
Sir Andrew Agnew (best known for his rigid addiction to
Lord's Day Observance) brought round to meet him George
Bull, the Evangelical curate of Bierly, Bradford, the most
active of that admirable group of West Riding clergymen
who were supporting the movement. They asked Ashley to
assume Sadler's place at its head, and to reintroduce the Bill
that had got stuck in the 1832 session. They told him that if he
was to decide to help them he must do so at once, in order to
get his oar in before Lord Morpeth, the member for the West
Riding, who was known to be about to introduce a Bill that
would not give them all they wanted. Ashley asked for a day

to think it over. He discussed it with his wife, meditated and prayed about it, and next day told them he would do it. Parson Bull and Richard Oastler, the irrepressible half-crazed 'Tory Radical' who did more than anyone to start the Ten-Hours' movement and keep its steam up, at once set about popularizing Ashley's name in the North; and Lord Morpeth, an old friend, noted with surprise and, no doubt, annoyance Ashley's unheralded interposition in a matter to which Morpeth, as member for that part of the country and a conscientious, good-hearted man, had given 'sedulous attention'. He wrote Ashley a civil little letter, explaining why he wanted to persist with *his* Bill, which proposed a compromise solution. Ashley replied in uncompromising style that he would support no Bill that did not meet the operatives' 'most just demands' for 'ten hours and no more, the total abolition of night-work, and eight hours only on Saturdays'.[1] He had committed himself; and even if he had not also been convinced that the merits of the case were on his side, he was the last man in the world to welsh on any cause he had publicly taken up.

But why had Ashley taken it up? He had never been near a factory in his life, he could hardly have told a millowner from an operative. His whole acquaintance with the question came from what he had read out of the report of Sadler's Committee and what he had been told by Sadler's friends – a mass of *ex parte* evidence, recognizable as such to men like Morpeth who knew something about it. Before committing himself so deeply, Ashley might have paused. He was, however, saved from an act so uncharacteristic by foreknowledge absolute. He had no doubt that he already understood the merits of the question. The illustrative details could be fitted later into their allotted places. All that mattered, in February 1833, was that he suddenly, unexpectedly, was offered an opportunity to expose and to defeat the class of men whom he had recently learnt to regard as the most sinister and odious in Britain – the millowners.

1 Hodder, i. 152, checked against the original at Castle Howard (series 2, book 15), which is a good deal longer but not significantly different.

Millowners looked like this to Ashley because they epitomized the many-sided revolution which British society was undergoing. Ashley disliked amost everything he knew about this revolution, and was quite ready to believe that everything he did not know was bad as well. His attitude was not uncommon among the more rurally minded of his party, and there was much in it to appeal to the more industrially and commercially minded ones too; if there had not been, they would not have remained Tories. It received its most persuasive expression in the later writings of Robert Southey – in those long articles for *The Quarterly Review* which he collected and published as *Essays Moral and Political* in 1832, and in his striking book *Sir Thomas More: or, Colloquies on the Progress and Prospects of Society*, which came out three years earlier. Ashley was deep in correspondence with Southey from 1831 onwards, and was undoubtedly much under Southey's influence. But he could have learnt to look at affairs this way without Southey's tutelage. Plenty of conservative writers besides Southey were during those same years making similar analyses of current economic, social, political and intellectual tendencies, and coming up with the same sort of findings. They differed as to details; but on general principles their unanimity was wonderful. They were generally gloomy, because they thought they saw a most unwholesome and dangerous sort of society emerging. Whether or not they agreed that society in 'the olden time' had been infinitely preferable – and Ashley, for one, doubted it – they all agreed about the present. Society ought to be stable, peaceful, harmonious, the lower orders looking up to the higher for protection, guidance and betterment, and the higher conscientiously providing it. Harmony and stability need not entail stagnation; society could be progressive, but progress should proceed in an orderly and equitable style, all orders enjoying its benefits. This was the ideal: aristocratic, paternalistic, community spirited, religious, and, however hard its more sensible exponents tried to devise its adaptation to modern conditions, fundamentally rural. It stood opposed to almost everything that was happening in early nineteenth-century Britain. Society was apparently fluid, disorderly, full of suspicions and hatreds; the lower orders were not getting the kindly authoritative help they needed, and were showing a dangerous new tendency to help themselves; there was progress of a kind, but only according to coarse materialistic criteria, and benefiting one section of the community at the expense of another. Over against their imaginary ideal, the Tory paternalists imagined they saw a reality that was torn by the conflict of oligarchy against democracy, individualistic, competitive, decreasingly religious, more and more urban. The new towns and cities were its worst parts. There, this specious hectic ruthless spirit of progress showed itself most out of control, the lower orders most depressed, the higher most heartless; there, Mammon reigned, and his high priests were the millowners – the 'millocrats', as some radicals called them.

It is not difficult to see why the millowners held this bad eminence in the early nineteenth century. They were by far the largest definable group of new-style industrialists, and most of the great success-stories of the early industrial revolution came from among them: the Arkwrights, Peels, Strutts, Marshalls and so on. Their works were conspicuous, compact (as those of their nearest rivals, the iron-masters, often were not), and always patently modern. They employed large numbers of women, 'young persons' and children *in factories* (about 260,000, in 1835), working under close supervision, or 'discipline', as their enemies liked to call it, to the rhythm of their great steam-engines or water-wheels; they were responsible for the first and most heart-breaking of all replacements of hand-work by machinery, that which slowly starved the handloom-weavers; some of the darkest and least forgotton episodes of late eighteenth-century history concerned their forerunners' use of infant pauper labour. For many reasons, therefore, they were notorious. It was not indeed reasonable or just, by the 1830s anyway, that they should have been so; but reason and justice have rarely been at more of a discount in British politics than between 1832 and 1846. British society was then profoundly disturbed and riven. Disraeli's description of it as 'the Two Nations – The Rich and the Poor' would have been more accurate if he had said 'Three', for the deepest rift of all was that between two sorts of 'rich': the prospering purposeful men of the new urban civilization, going to different schools and places of worship and entertaining different economic and political ideas from the still prospering traditional ruling classes with their mainly rural and agricultural interests, their still secure dominance in government, their attachment to the Established Church, and their even tighter attachment to agricultural protection, whatever newfangled free-trading theories might be applied to the rest of the economy. The Corn Laws thus appeared to most Conservatives and gentry as an indispensable bulwark to all they held dear; and so the Corn Laws became for the new urban men the standard symbol of all that thwarted and oppressed them, just as the millowner became, for the men of the old England, the standard symbol of all that was most hateful in the new.

Certainly from Southey – probably from other Tory writers – probably also from ordinary conversation with friends in the Commons and the new Carlton Club – Ashley learnt thus to regard the millowners, and to believe the worst of them. In a letter which Ashley must have received only a week or so before Agnew and Bull came round, Southey retailed a not wholly credible story about the heartlessness of John Marshall, the Leeds flax-spinning magnate who had unseated Sadler, and wrote, in all seriousness: 'I know not where the love of gain appears in more undisguised deformity than in a cotton-mill. . . . I know not how a cotton-mill can be otherwise than an abomination to God and man.' Southey (who seems also to have thought that Marshall's was a cotton mill) thought slave plantations much more defensible. A few weeks later he was averring that Moloch was 'a more merciful friend than Mammon. Death in the brazen arms of the Carthaginian idol was mercy to the slow waste of life in the factories.' Equally colourful language was the stock-in-trade of the Ten-Hours' orators; and Ashley joined in with a will. His speeches were fiery, his tours of the factory districts triumphal, his denunciations of the millowners unsparing. His Ten-Hours' friends, many of whom held radical political views, did not perhaps all clearly remark that his detestation of the millowners was not solely because of the inhumanities of their system. Ashley was no less concerned to counter their threat to his aristocratic and paternalistic social principles. 'I have done much', he wrote in 1841, 'in hope to conciliate the landed gentry in their [the operatives'] behalf, and approximate the parties who have common interests, and, "tell it not in Gath", a common enemy, the millowner!; he is not necessarily, but optionally so – he is the Jacobin of commerce' (22 June 1841) Not only the Jacobin, but the Jesuit. Ashley began to suspect the millowner's baleful influence even where he could not see it, just as he did with the Puseyites. 'Will the religious public, as it is termed, do anything for me?' he wondered when he began to clear decks for action against the coal proprietors

The 'secular' public is doing wonderfully – will *The Record?* I have long suspected the mill-owning connections of that paper; Seeley's letter of today confirms me. 'Hamilton, who has the most sway in the Record, has just married a mill-owner's daughter and started his carriage on the strength of that alliance. . . .' Thus the secret is out! The support of *The Record* on the factory question has been very rare, and always cold. No marvel! [16 May 1842.]

As time went by, Ashley's language about the millowners somewhat moderated; he discovered that some of them were actually model employers, and in favour of the sort of factory legislation he was trying to pass; he realized that Oastler was an enthusiast, and the Ten-Hours' movement little more friendly to his political ideals than the 'millocrats'; he took a growing interest in the facts. Facts, indeed, were never in short supply after the establishment of the factory inspectorate in 1833. But between facts and '*the* facts' there was, then as always, a great gulf fixed; and the gulf was particularly wide in this case because of the emotional involvement of the fact-finders. Their emotions sometimes led them to get their facts wrong, or draw false conclusions from them. But even when they were thinking accurately, emotion still came in. How should it not have done so, when beneath all their arguments about hours and conditions of labour, all their compassion and common sense, lay a titanic struggle between two great social and economic interests, battling for the soul of later nineteenth-century Britain? — and while the humanitarian concern for women and children overlay, in the minds of the adult male operatives who gave the Ten-Hours' movement its political sting, an instinctive rejection of the whole capitalist system? Battleground that it thus was for the most potent forces shaping modern Britain, illustrative as it was of much that was bad as well as of much that was worthy in human nature, the factory question still lacks a definite history. It is still a battle-ground of contending principles. Small wonder, then, that when it was a live issue, facts were countered by facts, passions met by passions — that generous sentiments, misunderstandings, and unfair judgments equally thrived — that good men lost patience with good men, while not so good men profited from their dissensions

Of the many good men involved in it, Ashley was certainly one of the best; and between 1833 and 1846 he was the most important. Ashley never toyed with important topics. His conscience and his temperament alike forbade him to. Either he deliberately left them alone, for others to deal with, or he gave himself wholly to them. The factory question was one to which he wholly gave himself From 1833 to 1840 it was his main political concern. From 1840 to 1846 (when, being temporarily out of Parliament, he gave over its conduct to John Fielden) he ran it alongside the growing number of other great social questions which he had seen to be related to it. Nor was 1846 by any means the end of his interest in it. If he seemed thereafter to play a less conspicuous part, it was only because by then other powerful public men had learnt — largely from him — to attend to it themselves, and because he himself had come to see it in a larger context. For ceasing to keep it on a pedestal, the smaller-minded Ten-Hours' men much abused him. He felt their ingratitude and spite keenly; but derived some consolation, no doubt, from the thought that his extended exertions were enabling hundreds of thousands of other, more helpless, toilers to

enjoy the same sort of legislative protection which the wool
and cotton operatives got not later than 1844.

From 1833 to 1844 Ashley was the operatives' parliamentary
champion. Whenever their question was being debated, he
was sure to take a leading part. Often he was responsible for
its being debated at all. His work began in March 1833,
when he introduced a Bill very much the same as Sadler's
except that it proposed stiffer penalties for peccant millowners. Its main points were to ban the employment of
children under nine, to limit the hours of work for under-
eighteens to ten a day or forty-eight a week, and to ban the
working of under-twenty-ones between seven p.m. and
six a.m.; its net effect, whether Sadler and Ashley realized
it or not, would have been to limit the adult workers' hours
to ten as well. It was held up during the spring, while a Royal
Commission reinvestigated the question, much more
thoroughly and dispassionately than Sadler's Committee had
done the year before. The Ten-Hours' men had angrily opposed
its appointment, vilified and obstructed its investigators, and
pretty clearly demonstrated that their vaunted concern for the
factory children was either emotional gas or a front for
deeper, disputable designs. The more telling, therefore, when it
appeared towards the end of June, was the Commissioners'
Report, comprehensively reviewing the workings of the factory
system so far as it affected children, and concluding that it
worked to their grievous disadvantage. The Commission found
little evidence of millowners' sadism and brutality; what there
had been of that earlier on had almost all disappeared; but
they found overwhelming proof of overwork directly causing
physical and educational harm – 'fatigue, sleeplessness and
pain . . . deterioration of the physical constitution, deformity,
disease, and deficient mental instruction and moral culture. . . .'
The rooms they worked in were all too often dirty, over-
heated, malodorous; dangerous moving parts of machinery,
especially the great leather belts that took power to the mach-
ines from the main shafts, were rarely boxed in; the older the
mill, the worse, generally, it was. To meet the necessities of this
appalling situation, the Commissioners made many re-

commendations, the mixed boldness, humanity and good sense of which was evident to anyone not primarily concerned with the hours of *adults'* work. They proposed a ban on children under nine, and an eight-hour day for under-thirteens, with an absolute prohibition of their working between ten p.m. and five a.m.; the Commissioners' idea was that these youngsters should be available in two shifts, and thus free for the part-time schooling they proposed as a condition of children's employment at all. To enforce these conditions and to help millowners adjust to them, the revolutionary suggestion was made of a permanent inspectorate. The Government introduced a Bill incorporating these recommendations, and moreover enforcing a twelve-hour day for 'young persons' between thirteen and eighteen. Ashley stuck out for his own Bill, but was handsomely beaten on a division. The Government's Bill then became law, after its educational clauses had been grievously mutilated by the House of Lords. No comparably important measure was to follow it till 1844.

The Factory Act of 1833 did not, as it turned out, work well. It was a more workable measure than Ashley's, if only because it had not the character, which his certainly had, of class legislation; and despite its practical failings, it was an Act of immense importance, if only for its establishment of the factory inspectorate, the copious annual reports of which faithfully chronicle its successes and failures as well as building up a mighty body of official information upon which better legislation could be based. But it did not work well. The Peers had seen to it that the education clauses should be worthless. Due enforcement of the other clauses was found to be next to impossible wherever magistrates chose to let the owners down lightly; as they did, often being owners themselves. The owners of country mills had two just grievances, in that their supply of child labour was inadequate to maintain a shift system, and that the difficulties placed in the way of making up lost time hit them peculiarly hard, dependent as they usually were on the vagaries of water-power. The Act certainly pressed much less hard on prosperous owners of big urban mills than on the

others. The less buoyant a proprietor's business, the narrower
his profit margin, the more was he bound to feel hurt by any
diminution of those profits. Some of the criticisms levelled at
the Act thus had substance. Most, however, had precious little.
Owners made difficulties where none existed, exaggerated
existing ones far beyond their merits. They allowed the cause
of the children to sink quite out of sight as they indulged
doctrinaire economic objections (fortified by the economist
Nassau Senior's convenient discovery that not less than 11½
hours had to be worked daily to gain the minimum reasonable
net profit of ten per cent), doctrinaire individualist objections,
and common resentments of every kind, the most defensive
of which was their indignation at being singled out from the
host of employers of child labour, others of whom treated
children worse. For the first couple of years they persuaded
the inspectors and the Government to sympathize with them.
Then in the later 1830s the issues began to clarify, and it was
seen that the millowners wanted to have their cake and eat
it too. Did not humanity and the public interest (interest, that
is, in having its working-class children growing up not wholly
illiterate and debilitated) demand that the millowners should
perhaps suffer a little loss of profit, be put to a little extra
trouble, submit to more effective inspection? Ought not the
Government to enforce laws that Parliament had made?
The Ten-Hours' movement, aiming at ten hours for adults
as well as children, might not commend itself to parliamentary
opinion; but if the limitation of women's and children's hours
simply could not be achieved without incidentally reducing
adult males' hours, was that to hold up the effective limitation
of children's and women's hours for ever? From 1836 these
and other awkward questions were more and more relentlessly
asked; and Ashley was foremost in asking them. In 1836 he
was prominent in opposition to a Government Bill that would
have diminished even further the effectiveness of the 1833
Act. Two years later he kept the question vividly before Parliament and the public when the Government was anxious to let
it drop, and ended up with a splendid motion of censure which
only failed, in quite a full house, by fifteen votes. Thus

badgered, by Ashley and his friends on one side, by their own inspectors on the other, the Government tried to improve the law in 1839. But when Ashley carried an amendment extending protection to children in silk and lace mills, the ministers, hard pressed from behind the scenes by the millowning lobby, made it a pretext for abandoning their Bill. So the 1830s ended with the 1833 Act still unamended on the statute book, and lamentably weak in operation. For this, Ashley was the least to blame.

In 1840 he did two very important things. First, he moved for a Select Committee 'to inquire into the operation of the Act for the Regulation of Mills and Factories'. Some such general view had become indispensable to further progress. The machinery set up in 1833 had broken down – the law disregarded, its agents the inspectors and their subordinate superintendents contemptuously defied, children neither protected nor educated as the Commons had intended. None of the interested parties was satisfied. The millowners still made moan, the 'short-timers' still clamoured for their uniform ten-hour day, the good men in between still sought a solution reasonably acceptable to masters and workers alike. Ashley's Committee went over the whole of the ground thoroughly, took evidence from representatives of each party, and after nearly a year published a report which unanswerably laid down the lines for further legislation.

Ashley's other gesture in 1840 was ultimately of even greater value. Just before the session closed, he demanded the setting up of a Royal Commission of Inquiry into Children's Employment in general. So far the humanitarians had been fighting on the one front of the textile industry. The reasons for starting there were sufficiently obvious. But Ashley's restless mind had for some time been worrying about other fields of juvenile employment. During his trips to the Midlands and the North to familiarize himself with the factory question he had looked beyond the horizons of the Ten-Hours' movement. He had been asking questions, reading widely, and biding his time. Now, judging that the public was ready, he initiated one of the most important public inquiries of the century, and in doing so cut from under their feet one of the millowners' main contentions: that they were not the only, nor the worst, exploiters of child labour. His arguments were powerful and statesmanlike.

Sir, I hardly know whether any argument is necessary to prove that the future hopes of a country must, under God, be laid in the character and condition of its children; however right it may be to attempt, it is almost fruitless to expect, the reformation of its adults; as the sapling has been bent, so will it grow. . . . Now, Sir, whatever may be done or proposed in time to come, we have, I think, a right to know the state of our juvenile population; the House has a right, the country has a right. . . . The first step towards a cure is a knowledge of the disorder. We have asserted these truths in our factory legislation; and I have on my side the authority of all civilised nations of modern times; the practice of this House; the common sense of the thing; and the justice of the principle. . . . It is right, Sir, that the country should know at what cost its pre-eminence is purchased. 'Petty rogues submit to fate, that great ones may enjoy their state.' The number I cannot give with any degree of accuracy, though I may venture to place them as many-fold the number of those engaged in the factories; the suffering I can exhibit, to a certain degree, in the documents before me.

He proceeded to do so, and thus gave Parliament its first taste of a brand of horrors with which it was soon to become painfully familiar. After showing in what manner children had to work in a wide variety of trades and industries, he rapidly surveyed the disastrous social consequences which must follow, and appealed to clergymen of every denomination 'to urge on the hearts of their hearers the mischief and the danger of these covetous and cruel practices'; reinforcing this, for 1840, most unusual oecumenical gesture, with a moving quotation from a recent address by the Archbishop of Rheims. At last he reached his peroration.

My first grand object is to bring these children within the reach of education; it will then be time enough to fight about the mode. . . . I am sure that the exhibition of the peril will terrify even the most sluggish and the most reluctant into some attempt at amendment; but I hope for far better motives. For my part I will say, though possibly I may be charged with cant and hypocrisy, that I have been bold enough to undertake this task, because I must regard the objects of it as being created, as ourselves, by the same Maker, redeemed by the same Saviour, and destined to the same immortality; and it is, therefore, in this spirit, and with these sentiments, which, I am sure, are participated in by all who hear me, that I now venture to entreat the countenance of this House, and the co-operation of her Majesty's Ministers, first to investigate, and ultimately to remove, these sad evils, which press so deeply and so extensively on such a large and such an interesting portion of the human race.[1]

Before considering the momentous consequences of the Children's Employment Commission (see page 115) we must return to the narrower front of the Ten-Hours' movement. Ashley presented his Committee's Report to the Commons in the middle of February 1841. Although he was very busy that spring (as, indeed, all that year) with the Jerusalem Bishopric project, he kept looking for an opportunity to introduce an improved Act; and he might have done so later that session, had not Melbourne's weary administration been beaten on 4 June on a motion of 'no confidence'. It was only beaten by one. But for two or three years it had been failing. Only Peel's determination to wait until the swing of the electoral pendulum should sweep the Whigs decisively away (and young Queen Victoria's determination to obstruct that sweeping as long as she could) had kept it going so long. But now the Whigs' hour had struck, and the curtain rose upon one of the most significant episodes of Ashley's life. The formation of a Conservative administration could not long be delayed; and Ashley did not mind the factory question being held up by as interesting an event as that. 'June 6th. – Trinity Sunday. Took the Sacrament as a fitting and comfortable preparation for the coming times of personal and political difficulty.'

The prospect of his own party's return to power pleased Ashley for several reasons. In general he preferred Tories to Whigs. Some Tories indeed he disliked, just as he quite liked many Whigs. Melbourne, Palmerston, Russell, Normanby and Morpeth had all at one time or another behaved decently

1. 4 August 1840. *Hansard*, 3rd series, lv. 1260–79.

towards him and helped achieve his objects; as all but old Melbourne, now taking his last bow, were to do again. But Ashley thought Whig political practice had latterly been very bad, with its catchpenny pandering to the radicals, its weakness towards the millowners, and its addiction to an undenominational latitudinarian sort of Christianity that was ultimately no better, however much less provoking, than Puseyism. This bad practice sprang from the underlying philosophy of Whiggism, which Ashley abhorred. His Toryism, he believed, was infinitely superior. Not that he was a 'good party man'. He had begun his political life as one, but the events of the early thirties, the friendship with Southey and so on, had taught him to be something bigger; he was a Conservative not because sticking to the Conservatives offered him power and success, not because he especially admired the Conservative leaders, but simply because he believed that the Conservatives' principles were sounder than the Whigs', and more conducive to a healthy state of society. His ideas of politics and of his place in politics as a Conservative did not commit him to that blind following of the leader which subscription to the Conservative party tends to induce in its members; nevertheless he seems so far to have doubted neither that his ideas and those of his nominal leaders sprang from a common social philosophy, nor that his political conduct during the thirties was anything but that of a good Conservative.

During the autumn of 1841 and the winter that followed, he was to learn the extent of his error. He received a painful shock, which caused a recasting of his ideas of his political role so thorough and permanent that he seems subsequently to have interpreted his earlier course in the light of it, and to have led Hodder to do the same. For it is impossible to believe that he did not expect Peel to give him a good place in his administration. Ashley had no grounds for supposing that Peel particularly liked him, nor, for that matter, was he sure he particularly liked Peel. 'Where is Peel's heart *now*?' he asked himself on the day of Parliament's dissolution. 'Is it set at the foot of God's throne . . . praying that he might become an humble instrument of His providence, laying aside all private interests, prejudices and carnal affections? I do not know . . .' (22 June 1841).[1] A few weeks later, after the general election had returned a solid Conservative majority, Ashley still did not know. He thought there was an

awful probability that it may not please God to render Peel an instrument of good to this nation. . . . He has abundance of human honesty, and not much of Divine faith; he will never do a dishonourable thing, he will be ashamed of doing a religious one; . . . a well-turned phrase of compliment, and eulogy from John Russell or Macaulay, will attract him more than 'Hast thou considered my servant Job?' Will he appoint Puseyite bishops? Will he elevate neological writers? Will he open his eyes, and expand his heart, to the mighty concerns of the present day, or will he lie entrenched in native coldness, fast bound with precedent and red tape? If so, the issue is final; if the reverse, the world lies before us, and we shall march, under God's banner, through the length and breadth of all lands, not in a spirit of conquest and ambition, but as the [moral?] sovereigns of His power, spreading religion and happiness around, and preparing the way for the restoration of His once loved People. [24 July 1841.]

Evidently, Ashley's plans for the new Government were not quite the same as Peel's. Such grandiose imperial themes, such heart-warming idealism, was quite alien to Peel's way of thinking; while as for God's 'once loved People', Peel was only prepared to spend valuable time thinking about *them* in so far as they might be made to figure in some sensible foreign policy, or be countenanced in the course of humouring touchy Evangelical supporters. Yet Ashley was no less worried than Peel about domestic dangers and, with the single exception of his addiction to the Ten-Hours' principle, looked to the same sort of remedies: church reform, religious education, the restoration of the 'just influence' of the landed gentry, the assimilation of the growing middle class to the gentry's traditional standards of social responsibility, the re-establishment of strong government after five years of feebleness. Here was a substantial body of shared Conservative con-

1 '. . . but sure I am,' he continued, 'that many are there for him; and grant, O blessed God, that mine may be there too!'

victions; and Ashley did not, in the summer of 1841, believe
that the firmness of his views about factory legislation would
involve his exclusion from Peel's government. Rather did he
believe that Peel could be persuaded to adopt the same views.
He was sure that Peel ought to do so. He knew that Peel
would not do so willingly, and was psychologically prepared
for the eventuality of Peel's absolute refusal:

He will succumb to the capitalists and reject my Factory Bill. . . .
My part is resolved, if Peel oppose me; nay, even if he does not
support me; I will surrender interest and ambition to the cause;
I will persevere in it, God helping me, through storm and sunshine;
I will commit all to Christ, and, trusting in Him, I shall never be
confounded. [27 August 1841.]

That this was largely rhetoric, and that he none the less
(however unreasonably) thought Peel would come the whole
way to meet him, was made clear a few days later, when Peel
(equally unreasonably) asked him to join the Government as
Treasurer to the Royal Household. It was not unreasonable
of Peel to expect Ashley to meet him half-way over the factory
question; but it was unreasonable to offer Ashley no better
a post than this. It marked a positive decline in status from the
junior positions he had held from 1828 to 1830 and in 1835.
Since then Ashley had become one of the most prominent,
active and useful of Peel's supporters. He had been mortified
when Peel had offered the same in 1839: 'I was thunderstruck.
Everything rushed before my mind: the trivialities of a Court
life, the loss of time, the total surrender of my political
occupations, and of all that an honourable ambition had
prompted me to hope for; instead of being a Minister, to
become a mere puppet . . .' (11 May 1839). He was even more
mortified now, at Peel's pressing on him 'a department in
which I could exhibit nothing good but my legs in white shorts'
(3 September 1841). Wholly unconvinced by Peel's arguments
that he would in fact perform a most valuable service by keeping the tone of the Court moral and pure, and determined
to preserve his freedom of action on the factory and all other
social questions, he declined office, and Peel went on without
him.

This was in some respects sad, but it appears to have been inevitable. Confronting each other here were two of the strongest-minded great men of the century. Each was capable of concession when it seemed right to concede; but neither was by nature of a conciliatory disposition, and they were at loggerheads over what they believed to be matters of principle. The Treasurership of the Household was no more than the pretext, the superficial occasion, of their disagreement. Peel no doubt thought that Ashley would be useful in the Household, but it is difficult not to believe, with Ashley, that Peel thought he would be a prickly colleague in an office that really mattered. ' I hear now', Ashley noted on 4 September 1841, 'that I was discussed for a variety of offices, Secretaryship for Ireland, etc., but Peel thought me "impracticable".' It is all too likely. Ashley's addiction to the factory question was not the whole of the matter. There was his religious enthusiasm too. Peel, an elderly man of scientific interests whose deep and unsophisticated latitudinarian sort of piety was coming to look somewhat old-fashioned, could get along well enough with Evangelicals – but what about an Evangelical of the Evangelicals? Clever young William Gladstone, 'the rising hope of the stern unbending Tories' as Macaulay called him, was also a religious and psychological puzzle to Peel; but he was young enough and, so far, politically orthodox enough to be manageable. Ashley was not manageable in the same way. Moreover – and this was the crux of the matter – Ashley had committed himself again and again to one side of a question which Peel could not help seeing the other side of. Tragically, they were not all that far apart. Peel thought that Ashley on the whole was right about the factories and their owners. His Government's policy, as he began to reveal it in 1842, brought upon him even grosser vilification from the millowners' leaders than had ever been visited on Ashley. But two principles stood between him and Ashley's view of the question. One was economic. Peel subscribed, albeit unhappily, to the orthodox economic theory of the day; he would after due consideration interfere, for their own and the nation's good, with women's and children's conditions of employment;

he would *not* interfere with those of adult males. The other principle was political and constitutional, and he only differed from Ashley in his application of it. Peel was not just a politician running an administration, he was also a constitutionalist trying to restore sound principles to the working of a constitution grievously disturbed by fifty years of change culminating in the Reform Act of 1832. To a thoughtful Conservative mind the effect of that disturbance had been to overweight the representative, 'popular' parts of the constitution as against the executive and 'aristocratic'. Parliament seemed to be in danger of becoming the instrument by which public opinion (gusty, inexperienced and irresponsible as it often was) directed government, instead of being the arena in which the king's government (with the stability and strength of semi-independence) approved itself to the king's subjects. There was no going back behind 1832, nor did Peel consider it desirable that government should ever get seriously out of step with public opinion. But there were several different ways of keeping in step, and two which Peel would *not* take were, first, to espouse a popular cause and promise specifically to attend to it when next in office, and, second, to give in to popular movements. So deeply was he impressed with the importance of this that he would even take pains to avoid the appearance of giving in to popular movements, when he was not in fact doing so. Here was Ashley, his hands as a prospective legislator tied by the specific pledges he had given to the short-timers, his *idée fixe* the passage of a Bill which would appear to place a premium on mass agitation. His mind set as it was, Peel could not possibly take Ashley into his cabinet.

Ashley, for his part, shared most of Peel's constitutional principles, but interpreted them after a more romantic style. Besides, he was more impetuous by nature and, although not in the least democratic, a bit of a demagogue. His political thought was less in terms of the constitution than Peel's, more in terms of conscience. When his conscience was aroused, he did not pause like Peel to consider the logical implications of his actions. In any case his campaign on behalf of the factory workers had seemed to him no more than a practical application of the paternalistic theory to which all Tories by definition adhered. He had announced to an oppressed class of fellow-countrymen his party's sympathy with their sufferings; he had urged them to support his party, and they had faithfully done so. He had acquired a certain popularity among them and influence over them, the nearest equivalent perhaps that could for the time being be achieved in the urban, industrial districts to the landowner's 'just influence' over his country-side; 'Depend upon it', he told Peel, 'I had a material influence over the return of the West Riding, and I know that I have conciliated thousands of hearts to our blessed Constitution' (3 September 1841). He had not sought this influence for himself, he had sought it on behalf of 'the cause of paternal and constitutional government', and his friends in the party cheered him on.

My pen would blush were I to detail the lofty, glowing, grateful praises I have received from M.P.s and the Carlton Club, for my noble efforts and my prodigious sacrifices to the state; for years I have accepted and believed them; but they have been redoubled during the last two or three months; none so loud as Graham, Hardinge and Goulburn, three members of the government from which I am excluded on account of the actions which they so much extolled. . . . How has Graham spoken in admiration of my influence as greater than any man's in the whole Empire! . . . Oftentimes has he urged me to expose the curses of the factory system in the House of Commons; nay, we had agreed that, if the Government proposed their Corn Law for discussion, he would exhibit the effect on the poor soils of England, and I, the evils which awaited the husbandmen who would crowd into the manufacturing towns! This is all very well! I and the operatives have sown the field, and Peel and his friends have reaped the harvest. . . . [4 September 1841.]

Ashley was writing under the influence of strong emotion, and it is not clear how far he was exaggerating the extent of the encouragement that Graham and the others had actually given him; but certain it is that he had gone on with the factory question believing that it was impeccable Toryism to do so, and that it need not be – surely *ought* not to be – a barrier to his attaining the high office for which, right up till September 1841, he inwardly yearned.

A barrier, however, it thus turned out to be. Ashley was mortified, Peel was at any rate sorry; neither was so mean as to let this unhappy disagreement prevent their co-operating on all the other questions that remained for the Conservatives to deal with, and Ashley stepped into the curious position he was to continue to hold for the next ten years or so, as a kind of unofficial, part-time member of the administration, working occasionally from the back-benches, lending respectability to the administrations he thus supported and saving them a good deal of trouble by seeing to the introduction and management of motions and Bills they approved. He was pleased to do this, for it fitted his notions of good government and it implied the pettiness of party rivalries. But he retained a perfect liberty to judge governments and their measures on their merits; and he set about Peel straight away, by writing to the secretary of the Yorkshire Short-Time Committee to say that since Peel would not commit himself to 'that measure which I consider . . . vital both to the welfare of the working classes and the real interests of the country', he – Ashley – had declined to accept office under him.

There was one more flurry before this unhappy incident was completely closed. These events of early September of course left Ashley in a state of acute sensitivity. Peel and Sir James Graham, the Home Secretary, for whom he now came to entertain a special dislike, would not give him the whole of what he wanted; he ran precipitately to the conclusion that they would give him nothing at all. This was unreasonable and unjust. They were very busy men, working out a pro-gramme of measures to suit the condition of a nation deep in economic depression and torn as terribly as nation ever has been by social and political hatreds. They had much to think about besides the measures to which Ashley was free to devote his mind; nevertheless Ashley's measures were on their agenda, and already by the end of the year Graham was writing very civilly to Ashley about the draft Factory Act he had found at the Home Office. He mentioned, *en passant*, that he was no Ten-Hours' man himself but showed sincere interest in the ques-tion and perfect willingness to settle it on the lines laid down by Ashley's Committee. Ashley, stickling for his ten-hour's formula, picked a quarrel with him and went on to press Peel for a definite answer: would the Government, or would it not, 'concede the prayers of the operatives for the further limitation of the hours of labour between the ages of thirteen and twenty-one?' Ashley ought to have known better than to try to bully Peel, who civilly but firmly declined to pledge himself to anything. Ashley tried another tack. Would he have the Government's support if he brought in a Ten-Hours' Bill himself? Peel simply repeated what he had said before. Ashley thereupon lost his temper and published a letter to the Short-Time Committees of Cheshire, Lancashire and Yorkshire, announcing that 'Sir Robert Peel has signified his opposition to the Ten Hours Bill'. He did not mention the fact that the Home Secretary was wrestling with the details of a far more comprehensive factory Bill than any of his precursors had thought practicable.[1]

The factory question got no further that session; Ashley had plenty of other work on hand – his Collieries Bill and the nation-wide lunacy inquiries – and the Government had its momentous fiscal and commercial reforms to get going, not to mention the 'plug plot' to handle during the summer. It revived early the following year. Ashley began it on 28 February 1843 with a fine speech urging the Government strenuously to consider some scheme of national education. He painted a terrifying picture of the way the children of the urban and industrial poor lived, and of the 'fearful multitude of un-tutored savages' they would turn into if they were left untouched by civilization and Christianity.

The early ages [he truly remarked] are of incalculable value; . . . every year of delay abstracts from us thousands of useful fellow-citizens; nay, rather, it adds them to the ranks of viciousness,

1 This letter was dated 2 February 1842. Two days later Ashley saw in the *Morning Post* 'the most violent and venomous article I ever read against any public man, directed against myself. Is it a "statement by authority"? I confess I think it breathes the spirit of a man mortally offended. . . . Was Peel the author, or the furnisher of the matter? or is it a Puseyite article, paying me off for my resistance to Mr Williams? It is cleverly done, malignant but ingenious' (4 February 1842).

of misery and disorder. So long as this plague-spot is festering
among our people, all our labours will be in vain; our recent
triumphs will avail us nothing – to no purpose, while we are rotten
at heart, shall we toil to improve our finances, to expand our commerce, and explore the hidden sources of our difficulty and alarm.
We feel that all is wrong, we grope at noonday as though it were
night; disregarding the lessons of history and the Word of God, that
there is neither hope nor strength, nor comfort nor peace, but in a
virtuous, a 'wise and understanding people'. . . .

Graham generously expressed the House's concurrence in
Ashley's sentiments, and said that he was about to introduce an
improved Factory Bill that would, he hoped, meet Ashley's
requirements. This Bill was presented a week later. Its protective clauses were more extensive than those of any previous
Bill, but public opinion focused at once on its education clauses,
which were even more noteworthy. The part-time schooling
intended by the 1833 Act had sadly flopped, through lack of
schools, evasions of the Act or nominal compliances with it
that came to the same useless thing in practice. Graham and
the inspectors now intended that wherever there were factories there should be schools for the factory children and
their younger brothers and sisters; the schools were to be
partly paid for out of the poor rates, and to be managed by
boards of seven trustees. About the composition of these
boards great argument followed. The Dissenters with some
justice objected to the predominance they gave to the Established Church, and petitioned en masse against them. Graham
went a long way to meet the Dissenters. With much less justice
they continued to object so violently that, despairing of a
harmonious solution, he gave up the education clauses entirely. Ashley was much disheartened. He did not blame one side
more than the other; the Established Church was being asked
to make very large concessions, the Dissenters had much
Establishment insolence to repay; he blamed both equally
for indulging their mutual hatreds and suspicions at the
expense of 'the vast body of neglected children'. His verdict
seems fair enough. Modern descendants of neither party have
much cause to take pride in a dispute that held up the develop-

ment of a national schools system for nearly thirty years, and helped to keep hundreds of thousands of children in brutish ignorance.

By the time the education clauses were withdrawn, the session was far advanced. Ashley tried to harry Peel and Graham into going on with what was left of the Bill. They half-succumbed to his importunity, but time ran out. Early in 1844, however, Graham re-entered the arena with a Bill the protective clauses of which went slightly further than those of the preceding year. His main proposals were now a 6½-hour day for the eight to thirteens, worked either before or after lunch with three hours' school in the other half of the day; a maximum of twelve hours for the thirteen to eighteens and (this was new) *all* women, to be worked between six a.m. and eight p.m. Many other clauses were expressly designed to make sure the Act really worked. Graham was not selling out to the millowners, as Ashley persistently alleged. His Bill, with its strict prohibition of working late hours to catch up lost time (except in wholly water-powered mills), its promise of more regular and authoritative inspection, was as distasteful to them on their side as it was to Ashley on his. Graham was attempting a middle course, unlikely to please any party. He agreed with Ashley that many millowners were ruthless and socially irresponsible. He also agreed with the better millowners that Ashley was hot-headed and prone to exaggeration. He therefore presented an adamantine front to Ashley's repeated attempts to reduce the overall working-time for women and young children from between six a.m. and eight p.m. to between six a.m. and six p.m.; which, allowing for meals, would have given *them* a ten-hour day, and consequently (since they formed so large a proportion of the whole labour force) the adult males too.

Ashley never showed better parliamentary form than in these debates of 1844. His big speeches were eloquent, argumentative, and stirring; deeply involved though his feelings were, they were perfectly under the control of his intelligence; and, fortified by his moral disapproval of the heads of the Government, he played the part of opposition leader to perfection. He went to great pains, moreover, to found his opposition on a broad national base. By this time he was recognizing not only that some industrialists were thoroughly good men, but also that industrialists had much justice on their side when they counter-attacked by saying that life down on the farm was often no better for the labouring man than life in the town. He was, in fact, coming to see the factory question in a wider perspective. It was merging into the general question of how the less gifted, fortunate, or self-reliant of the lower orders were to be protected from the dreadful consequences of weakness, failure or redundancy. More than any other influential public man he was calling the nation's mind, rousing the nation's conscience, to face this terrific question; and the more conscious he became that this was his onerous task, the more anxious did he become to clear himself of the charge of partisanship. Hence the extraordinary courage with which, at the end of November 1843, he took the opportunity of a big agricultural banquet at Sturminster to call the landowners and farmers of his own county to a higher sense of social responsibility and a greater generosity towards their poor – a call which lost him much local popularity and involved him in a fierce dispute with his father.[1] Hence also the magnificence of his denial that he was only aiming

to exalt the landed and humiliate the commercial aristocracy. . . . If you think me wicked enough, do you think me fool enough for

1 See Hodder, i. 522, 11 December 1843. The top paragraph continues: 'Said not a word. Defence exasperates him. Could not but think that £900 last year for a hot-house, £600 for game, and £800 for a farm-house (which was wholly unnecessary, at least just now) would have enabled him to afford more than enough for these indispensable uses. . . .' His speech attracted much attention, and the Anti-Corn Law Leaguers, whose charges he was trying to answer, turned it deftly to their own purposes. 24 December 1843: 'Someone sent me this morning a copy of the *Manchester Guardian* (millowners' paper) – very malignant – likens me to "Red Mr Stephens" – well done! It will next liken me to Nadir Shah. It is nuts to the manufacturers to have a groundwork for misrepresentation against the landlords; the state of "the majority" of the labourers in the county of Dorset! ring the changes on *one* sentence in my speech, drop the context, and omit all the others. This is the true, manly, leaguer style! Like Hezekiah I spread it all before the Lord.'

such a hateful policy? Can any man in his senses now hesitate to believe that the permanent prosperity of the manufacturing body . . . is essential, not only to the welfare, but absolutely to the existence, of the British Empire? No, we fear not the increase of your political power, nor envy your stupendous riches. 'Peace be within your walls, and plenteousness within your palaces!' We ask but a slight relaxation of toil, a time to live, and a time to die; a time for those comforts that sweeten life, and a time for those duties that adorn it; and, therefore, with a fervent prayer to Almighty God that it may please Him to turn the hearts of all who hear me to thoughts of justice and of mercy, I now finally commit the issue to the judgment and humanity of Parliament.

Ashley did not, in 1844, succeed in converting Graham's Bill (a very good one of its kind) into a Ten-Hours' one; but he did succeed in hastening the day of a Ten-Hours' Bill, by carrying the House with him on two successive votes, and making it necessary for Peel and Graham to restore party discipline and their own authority by threatening to resign unless their Twelve-Hours' Bill was preferred. The threat worked, and these votes were duly rescinded. But such extraordinary doings did nothing to enhance Peel's popularity in his party; and Disraeli was to make much capital out of the incident when he set about the political assassination of Peel a year later. Graham's unpopularity was already so great that his share in the thwarting of the House could scarcely increase it; yet he too managed to draw new odium on himself, by suggesting a likeness between Ashley and Jack Cade, a suggestion at once immortalized by the greatest political cartoonist of the century. Altogether, Ashley had dominated the session; and after it a Ten-Hours' Bill could not long be delayed.

It was to come in 1847. It was not Ashley's fault that it came no sooner. He was not the man to let grass grow under his feet. Armed with the reports of the Children's Employment Commission, in 18 February 1845 he thought he might venture to introduce a Bill to extend protection to children employed in calico print-works, where the work was often singularly tiring and unhealthy. Again he emphasized his new theme of universal concern, using his opponent's argument that things were bad for labouring children everywhere to prove that children should everywhere be protected.

My opponents, on the first introduction of the Ten-Hours' Bill sent me to the collieries; when I invaded the collieries, I was sent to the print works; from the print works I know not where I shall be sent, for can anything be worse? . . . Sir, it has been said to me, more than once, 'Where will you stop?' I reply, without hesitation, 'Nowhere, so long as any portion of this mighty evil remains to be removed.' I confess that my desire and ambition are to bring all the labouring children of this empire within the reach and opportunities of education – within the sphere (if they will profit by the offer) of happy and useful citizens. . . . I fear nothing but defeat.[1]

The bill got through without much difficulty.

A twelvemonth later he tried the Ten-Hours' Bill again; but by then the Corn Laws crisis was in full swing, and since he agreed with Peel that they ought to go he felt obliged, as a man of honour, to give his agricultural constituency the chance to reject him.[2] They took it, and he was out of Parliament until the summer of 1847. This Bill of 1846 was therefore looked after by another and hardly less great reformer, John Fielden, who as an advocate of the measure had the advantage of being himself the owner of one of the biggest cotton factories in the country. Peel and Graham still resolutely opposed it, but the degree to which it had commended itself to public opinion since its last airing appeared in the slenderness of the majority by which they threw it out: only ten now, where it had been 138 two years before. One year more, and it was through. Fielden's Ten-Hours' Act became law of 8 June 1847. Ashley noted with particular pleasure that thirteen bishops voted for it.

Ashley's activities in the field of industrial legislation were dominated by his connexion with the Ten-Hours' movement:

1 *Hansard*, 3rd series, lxxvii. 638–56.

2 Questions of political morality are of all moral questions the most difficult to judge. One wonders whether the Hammonds bore this and many similar decisions of Ashley's in mind (e.g. his persistent refusal of office so long as Peel refused to support the Ten-Hours' Bill) when censuring him for letting 'power play with his principles'. See the paragraph on the 'Arrow' incident of 1857 in chapter 16 of their book.

but an even greater achievement than the eventual passage of
the Ten-Hours' Act (Ashley's, in all but name) was the way
he had broadened the industrial issue as the years went by,
and made the public realize that what it had to deal with was
not just a local trouble of the Lancashire and Yorkshire
textile operatives, but a dangerous disorder of the social
system that demanded recourse to first principles of social
and political theory as well as specific alleviation. Ashley
hammered this lesson home whenever he got the chance.
The textiles trade was only the broadest of his industrial
sounding-boards. There were many others. 'Climbing-boys' –
the wretched little lads used to sweep chimneys, and so often
maimed or murdered in the process – never ceased to haunt
him; he promoted legislation to protect milliners and dress-
makers; he secured the appointment of a second Children's
Employment Commission, upon the reports of which were
founded the Acts of 1864 and 1867 which at last brought the
whole juvenile, and most of the female, industrial labour
force (and, through Shaftesbury's special intervention, the
women and children of the agricultural gangs) under Parliament's protection; he had brickfield workers brought under
the same protection a few years later. But the most striking
of this series was one of the first. It occurred in 1842, the first
(and, alas! almost the only) fruit of the Children's Employment Commission he had caused to be appointed in 1840. Its
first report was on mines and collieries. It caused a sensation;
'I hear that no such sensation has been caused since the first
disclosure of the horrors of the slave trade,' noted Ashley;
'God, go before as in thy pillar of a cloud!' (24 May 1842).
Of all sections of the labouring classes, the mining communities
were the most self-contained, the least generally known about.
Hardly anyone who did not actually live among them had
realized that women were employed in many mines, children –
often very young ones – in almost all. What this employment
meant was now made distressingly clear. The public mind
became at once haunted by the spectres of half-naked women
and girls on all fours hauling trucks along passages too low
for ponies, or carrying baskets of coal up shaky vertical

ladders: bastards begotten and babies aborted in these infernal regions; girls and boys beaten and bullied by the brutal colliers who were their direct employers; and, most terrible, the youngest children of all keeping lonely vigil by the trap-doors which it was their task to open and shut, open and shut, for ten, twelve or even more hours at a stretch. Such horror was excited by these 'mining abominations', as Peel himself called them,[1] that Ashley had no difficulty in rushing a Bill through the Commons, despite the coal-owners' demand for a Select Committee of Inquiry instead. Things were more difficult in the colder climate of the Lords, where the proportion of coal-owners was much higher, and where, said Ashley, 'property is always the dominant question' (8 July 1842). Lord Devon took charge of it for him; many peers, including the Duke of Wellington, spoke against it, and perhaps only the clamour of public opinion induced them to pass it at all; only three bishops (one of them, Stanley) bothered to see it through Committee, and it came back to the Commons sadly mutilated. What followed when the Duke next met Ashley was marvellously characteristic of both parties. 'Strange to say of so great a man, but never did impudence go beyond that of the Duke of Wellington who expressed a belief to me that "I was satisfied with what has been done to my bill in the H. of Lords." I told him, "just the reverse" ' (1 August 1842). But it was a beginning and, indeed, it was quite a tough one. Boys under ten, and all females, were barred from underground work. Safety regulations were enforced for the first time, and – vital provision! – an inspectorate appointed. The mineowners loathed it. Let Ashley's be the last word.

August 8th. – Took the Sacrament on Sunday in joyful and humble thankfulness to Almighty God for [this] undeserved measure of success. . . . *Novus saeclorum nascitur ordo ?* . . . The more I labour, the more I see of labour to be performed, and vain at the last will be the labour of us all. Our prayer must be for the Second Advent, our toil 'that we be found watching'.

1 Letter of 16 June 1842. British Museum Additional Manuscripts, 40483, fos. 70–1.

5

WOE TO HER THAT IS FILTHY AND POLLUTED, TO THE OPPRESSING CITY! – [Zeph. iii, 1]

FOR the second half of his long life Lord Shaftesbury was at war with 'the city'. Not the city of the financiers; he would probably have been at war with that too, had he not other preoccupations; but the city as the men of the early nineteenth century knew it, the great new social phenomenon of their age – bustling, crowded, smelly, dirty, and growing huge and ugly, like Frankenstein's monster: growing perceptibly, day by day, as land values rose, new houses sprouted, older houses were heightened, empty spaces became filled with whatever buildings promised the richest returns – offices and warehouses here, tenements and gin-palaces there: growing hectically and unmanageably as cities had never grown before, far beyond the power of the existing local government authorities to control them, far beyond most men's capacity to imagine how they might be controlled.

This rapid growth was felt and, in proportion as its social consequences became better known and understood, feared, from the late eighteenth century onwards. Places like Leeds, Glasgow, Manchester, Edinburgh, Sheffield, Birmingham, Liverpool and Nottingham began to turn into cities of the new nineteenth-century type. But none of them approached, as none of them has ever approached, the size of London. About 1800 there were already a million people living in London.[1] No other city was yet over the 100,000 mark. Edinburgh, Glasgow and Liverpool were over it by the time the second national census was taken, in 1811; Birmingham and Manchester had joined them by 1821. These and similar cities' rates of growth were among the fastest in the country, and far exceeded that of the metropolis. But their growing

1 i.e. in the area once covered by the L.C.C., which was approximately the 'greater London area' of the time.

pains were only those which London had experienced earlier on; indeed, the ruling upper classes first had their attention called to the existence of the new urban problem when they began to see in the new cities the same alarming symptoms of political and moral disorder as had thitherto been considered London's bad peculiarity. By about 1820 they were wide awake to this new danger. But they were only aware of its moral and political aspects, and only able to conceive of corresponding cures: churches and clergymen, Sunday schools, policemen and prisons. Only a very insignificant group of pioneers of public health and local government reform was aware that its root causes – and dangers – lay deeper. Since the 1780s these men had been conducting local surveys and promoting piecemeal legislation. Now, about 1830, they began to form a common platform, to pool information and draw up plans for handling the urban problem on a national and fundamental scale. Such plans could not come to anything until the general public's defences of ignorance, indifference and superficial diagnosis were broken down. This break-through came apparently in 1842, when the greatest of these early reformers, Edwin Chadwick, published his *Report on the Sanitary Condition of the Labouring Population.* Like the contemporaneous first report of Ashley's Children's Employment Commission, it caused something of a sensation; and the few wise and good public men who had already been trying to get Parliament to face up to the urban problem in its proper depth were gladdened to feel a breeze of public opinion beginning to blow up behind them.

Ashley seems to have become aware of the city about this time. He must have known about Chadwick's Sanitary Report, and within a few years he was showing a highly intelligent and courageous understanding of the sanitary foundations of urban life. But at first his interest was rather in the human problems of the poorest poor, problems that were not primarily those of the conditions of employment (most of them in any case never had more than intermittent, casual employment) but the conditions and difficulties of living at all.

For the early Victorian city was extraordinarily unfriendly

to the poor. It was trying all the time to tip them over the
edge of ordinary poverty into the abyss of hopeless, helpless
poverty. Ordinary poverty was bad enough for at any rate
the unskilled workers. It meant long hours and small pay for
every member of the family who could earn anything. A
miner might send his children down the mine, a weaver might
send his to the factory, to help pay for gambling and beer or
to purchase the trimmings of social ascent, but for poor unskilled people in the city, where rents and food costs both were
high, every penny was a matter of survival or sinking – until or
unless you gave up struggling to survive. Rents were high
because city ground was so valuable; ground and rents were
cheaper on the outskirts, of course, but normally you could
not live there because you had to live within quick walking
distance of the chance of work. Because rents were high,
you could not afford much room to live in. Even well-paid
skilled men, before the era of the workmen's trains, might
find it hard to live 'respectably', with their boy children and
girl children in different bedrooms. The artisans at Maudslay
and Fields in Lambeth, making the best marine steam-engines
in the world, were living in the sort of narrow cramped little
cottages that passed as slums in Lancashire. Yet they were
among the *élite* of the labouring class, much nearer the lesser
white-collar workers and trades-people than they were to 'the
poor'. The London poor lived in much worse places than
Jurston and Hooper Streets, Lambeth. They lived in older,
squalider rows of cottages that had once been just suburban,
or in the flimsy houses that had been more recently crammed
into the still vacant spaces of such areas, turning them into
thickets of courts and alleys. They lived in tenements run
up in the gardens and backyards of once prosperous properties
that had now run down. They lived in 'rookeries': big old
houses converted into warrens of one-room and two-room
dwellings; rickety, unsanitated noisy fire-traps, hideous in
daylight and stygian at night, like Tom All-Alone's and
Jacob's Island. They lived in shacks and cabins in the shanty-
towns that had their brief, inglorious existences on the less
eligible low-lying suburban lands until values reached a point

that made it worth some developer's while to drain it. They lived in what were known as common lodging-houses; of which more anon.

These were the characteristic slums of early Victorian London: messier, closer, dirtier far than their later nineteenth-century successors or the more recently built rows of cottages in the East End, which are, in general, the 'Victorian slums' that still survive and shock us. They were horrible to live in, fraught with perils of every kind: foul water, dirty food, bad drains or no drains at all, rubbish rarely removed, police rarely seen, crime and drunkeness endemic. It was terribly easy to find yourself slipping down into these slums. A father or mother dead or disappeared, drunken or witless or lazy – a breadwinner crippled – a job lost and no character given – a set of tools or a street-barrow stolen – an infant too many – a week's unemployment (from whatever cause) too much – and inexorably there followed the failure to pay the rent, the eviction, the move to humbler, nastier quarters, with little hope of ever regaining the tenuous independence once lost. *Facilis descensus Averno, sed regredi* . . . it could not be done! If you could not get out yourself, who would give you a hand? Nobody in authority would: unless you became a public nuisance. Merely being a mobile source of disease or moral contagion, an illiterate, imbecile or brutish being apt to multiply its kind, was not yet a title to be regarded as a public nuisance. You could, in the 1830s, only qualify as a public nuisance by being a cut-throat, pickpocket or burglar, and being caught: or by being, for example, a very young lost child, or by collapsing from hunger or sudden illness or advanced pregnancy in a public place. Then indeed somebody, from an unsympathetic sense of duty, would help you to the police station or 'the parish'; from whence you might be forcibly conveyed down the appropriate channels, either (if it was the police station) to the hulks, the Antipodes or the gallows; or (if it was the parish) to the workhouse baby-farm, infirmary, casual or lying-in ward, as the circumstances of your case directed. Of course the workhouse-door was always open, to anyone who chose to apply. No one in Britain

in the 1830s needed to die wholly uncared for. The parish –
and, after 1834, the union[1] – was responsible for the relief of
destitution, and would provide a shaky minimum of medical
care where it seemed to be urgently needed. But you had to go
and get it, or, if you were too sick to move, to get somebody
to get it for you; and when you got it, it was pretty sure to be
of so spartan and severe a character as to make it distasteful
to all, repulsive to most. The poor kept away from the
workhouse as long as they could.

Upon this dark official scene shone, sporadically, the light
of private charity. 'The parish' was not quite the poor person's
only resource. Besides the workhouse (which is what 'the
parish' meant among the poor) old parishes usually had
certain exiguous charities – doles of bread, money, fuel,
clothing – distributed at stated intervals by churchwarden,
curate or clerk. There was a variety of almshouses and
hospitals into which the most respectable and presentable of
the poor might get admittance. There were charitable agencies
of all kinds run by voluntary societies: dispensing medicine,
soup, religious literature, cast-off clothing, good advice, and
even (after particularly careful inquiries) cash. These multi-
farious charities, which multiplied unceasingly through the
first two-thirds of the nineteenth century, must have done
much to sustain the flicker of life in many frames from which
it would otherwise have flown. One cannot behold their vast
collection and application of money and believe otherwise.
Yet they only alleviated the problem. They could not cure it.
For one thing their sights were set too high; they mostly
treated poverty, as did the new Poor Law for that matter, as
in the main a moral problem – not the economic one which it
began to be seen as towards the end of the century. For another
they were mostly, before the 1830s at any rate, far too static
and superior; they tended to wait for the needy to come to
them and sue *in forma pauperis*; they left the searching-out of
the needy to be done by the parish clergy, who were completely
baffled by the scale and danger of the search, if willing to

1 i.e. the union of parishes for poor-law purposes, created by the Poor
Laws Amendment Act of 1834.

undertake it at all. And, in any case, the problem was strictly insoluble. Not even a more lavish and perceptive apparatus of public policies and private remedies – a provision unimaginable at that date – could have done much to handle a problem so huge and ugly, the simple product of centuries of political freedom and property-rights, and of a recent sudden economic revolution. Such a situation was chronically desperate; and such was the situation with which Ashley began to involve himself in the early forties.

What first worried Ashley was the hopelessness and helplessness of the poorest poor. For the ordinary poor, of course, he was sorry; but nothing in their situation seems particularly to have moved him. There always had been poor, he knew; he did not doubt that there always would be. It was the duty of the upper orders of society to alleviate the necessary hardships of poverty. Employers should give fair wages and take a personal interest in their employees. The State should maintain a decent system of poor relief, a basic protection for the poor against the accidents of unemployment and illness; and Ashley accepted the newly reformed Poor Law as in principle adequate to this task, although he criticized some aspects of its administration.[1] Every reasonably prosperous Christian ought, he believed, to feel the same responsibility for the use of his money as for the use of his abilities and social position, and view the condition of the poor with humane and intelligent sympathy. Ashley's campaigns on behalf of the textile workers and yearnings to improve the lot of the Dorsetshire labourers show to what courses of action he conceived his responsibilities towards the 'ordinary poor' obliged him. But there were limits to what could be done – limits, perhaps, to what should be done – for them. It was no good giving lavish optimistic

1 It was the medical deficiencies of the poor law that principally disturbed him. On 5 March 1844 he persuaded the Commons to set up a Select Committee to investigate certain alleged cruel treatments of sick paupers. Four years later he was less successful in urging Parliament to insist on greater security for poor law medical officers and more consideration towards female paupers having first babies. For his suggestion that unmarried females should be treated as considerately in childbirth as married, he was accused of encouraging vice, etc., etc.

ideas to poor people who were never going to be anything but poor: no good either to let them think that anything but hard work and inflexible virtue would keep them going at all. Socialism appalled Ashley. He would have nothing to do with anyone who was at all that way inclined, and got terribly excited when he understood (or *mis*understood his Evangelical publisher friend R. B. Seeley to 'avow himself hostile to the present mode of descent of landed property' and to 'express his desire to break down families by piecemealing their estates'.[1] The *soi-disant* Christian Socialism of Maurice and Kingsley left him cold. *His* response to the threatened revolution of 1848 was to persuade Prince Albert and a cortège of gorgeous grandees to come with him on a tour of some St Giles's slums and to make a speech at the Labourers' Friend Society afterwards. 'Aye, truly', he rejoiced, 'this is the way to stifle Chartism. . . . The aristocracy, after a long separation, are re-approaching the people; and the people the aristocracy. Oh Cobden, Bright, and all that dismal crew, you will be crushed in the friendly collision!' His attitude towards the 'ordinary poor' seems to be fairly epitomized in the speech he made in 1872 at the foundation of the Shaftesbury Park Estate in Wandsworth – a 'workmen's city' built mainly with workmen's money by the semi-philanthropic Artisans', Labourers' and General Dwellings Company. They were building it, he told them, 'on the very best principles . . . the great principle of self-help, and the great principle of independence. By independence, I mean without any other assistance than that which every man has a right to receive from his fellow man – sympathy and kind aid – and that is what every man, great or small, stands in need of from another.'[2]

1. 8 September 1842: Ashley was especially upset because Seeley had been helping with the campaign against Isaac Williams, and Ashley had always maintained the Tractarians were malignantly mistaken in accusing their opponents of, *inter alia*, political radicalism. 'The discovery that Seeley's plans of amelioration are to issue in a social revolution, will greatly confirm their assertions and extend their party. God be with us! . . .'

2. *The Times*, 5 August 1872, p. 6c. He went on: 'You have founded the workmen's city upon your own efforts and by your own contributions,

Independence and self-help – the central virtues of Victorian respectability. Ashley valued them as much as anybody. He would do nothing to sap them. But, unlike too many of his contemporaries, he recognized that not all the independence and self-help in the world could save some of the poor from wretchedness and fatal decline. Some were so weak and help-less that they needed all the help they could get; and even the toughest might find their efforts unavailing in the face of ad-verse physical circumstances. Ashley understood that the criminality, disease and viciousness that marked many of the very poor was not their own fault. It was because he ap-preciated so clearly the force of environment, because he was not blinded to it by obsession with the moral and religious aspects of the problem, that Ashley earned such a distinguished place among the leaders of the Victorian battle with the city. His activities in this field fall into two categories: social rescue work and public health reform. Let us deal with them in turn.

The rescue work that first engaged Ashley's attention held it to the last: the Ragged Schools movement and its many more permanent offshoots. Ragged Schools were schools for children so dirty, verminous, violent and primitive that none of the ordinary primary schools run by the Church of England's National Society or the undenominational British and Foreign Schools Society would take them, even if they offered them-selves for taking. Such children by definition had bad parents, exceedingly poor parents, or no parents at all. In all big cities there were plenty of them. In London there were, in 1848, perhaps thirty thousand. They were a tough lot, for weaklings early succumbed in such an environment as theirs. They occupied their days and filled their bellies as best they could.

---

and for the great and wise purpose of advancing your social position and bodily health as well as your intellect and general prosperity. The domiciliary condition of the people involves health, comfort and happiness. It also involves contentment, and people who are contented always give a Government less trouble than those who are not. When men are contented, they become excessively reasonable, and employer and employed find that their interests are identical. They must hold together, and by united action give force to progress.'

Ashley told the Commons that they might be classed 'as street-sweepers, vendors of lucifer-matches, oranges, cigars, tapes and ballads; they hold horses, run on errands, job for "dealers in marine stores" – such is the euphonious term for receivers of stolen goods, a body of large influence in this metropolis, without whose agency juvenile crime would be much embarrassed in its operations'.[1] They ran up criminal records that would not have disgraced much more experienced individuals; Thomas Miller, for example, twelve years of age and four feet two inches in his bare feet, when he appeared at Old Bailey in 1849 had had at least seven convictions, spent at least thirty months in prison, and been whipped twice. When not at work or play – and of course they were often up very late, catching the crowds as they came out of the pubs or, on Sundays, the evening meetings – they disappeared to the hovels, rookeries and lodging-houses which were their titular homes, or to the holes and corners where unwanted, unattached beings like themselves could keep out of the way of the rain and the police: under tarpaulins on barges or carts, in unused brick-kilns (much coveted, as often retaining some warmth from their last firing), in half built or ruinous houses, under bridges and the arches of railway viaducts. Ashley knew of a lad 'who, during the inclement season of last winter, passed the greater part of his nights in the iron roller of Regent's Park'.

Such children – 'wastrel children', as Ashley often called them; 'derelict children', as they were referred to by another of the men who set about rescuing them, John Fegan – were at least a nuisance and menace. Shopkeepers and costermongers lost heavily from their depredations. They were a natural nursery for the burglars and thugs that fanned out at night from their dark quarters in Westminster, Holborn, Clerkenwell and Bermondsey to make uneasy the slumbers of prosperous householders in Bayswater, Pimlico, Peckham and Dulwich. They were dangerous and detestable; they were also pathetically human and, to begin with at any rate, very young. No one quite knows who first ran a ragged school for these

1. 6 June 1848. *Hansard*, 3rd series, xcix. 432.

children. Perhaps it does not matter. What does matter is that by the 1830s ragged schools of one kind and another were turning up in most big cities, and most of all in London. Sometimes they were run by paid agents of charitable in-individuals or societies, sometimes by working-class philan-thropists themselves; usually they were conducted with a religious aim to pluck brands from the burning as well as the common-sense aim of reducing the criminal population. The metropolitan ones that Ashley came across in 1843 were run by the London City Mission. He responded to a notice in *The Times* appealing for funds for the school in Field Lane, Saffron Hill, and quickly became the public and parliamentary champion of the movement which took shape, in 1844, as the Ragged School Union. The annual prize-giving of this society became, like the May meeting of the C.P.A.S., one of his resounding regular public appearances.

It was the missionaries of the L.C.M. and the teachers of the R.S.U. who first revealed to Ashley how the city dealt with its poor;[1] and his familiarity with this fearful business grew *pari passu* with the R.S.U.'s activities. Under their tuition he penetrated the darker courts and alley-ways where no man in his senses would normally go without a bodyguard of policemen. He saw how the very poor lived in their own homes. He saw sights that he never forgot, sights that he would later in the century recall to show that although things were still bad, they were not nearly as bad as they had been. He had some strange experiences. The strangest, he thought, was when he took the chair at a thieves' meeting. One of the City Missionaries, Thomas Jackson, a patient, discreet and saintly man who had gained complete acceptance in his criminal quarter, arranged a secret meeting one night at which Ashley

1 In later life he used to recall the shock he had when, at Harrow, he one day ran into a pauper's drunken funeral, and to trace from it his philanthropic career. A plaque was subsequently placed there to com-memorate it. No doubt the sight did shock him; and very likely it did leave some mark on his mind. But there is no evidence of its having had the profound influence he came to read back into it, nor of his having had any first-hand acquaintance with London's slums before he was forty.

could come face-to-face with about four hundred crooks. Jackson began by reading the story of the thieves crucified alongside Jesus; then he asked them all to kneel, while he led in prayer; Ashley next asked some of them to tell him about themselves, before he told them, tactfully, how he thought they might escape into a better mode of life. This was, surely, an extraordinary occasion! But it was not his only such encounter, although it certainly impressed him the most. Twenty years later, when he was nearly seventy, he went to another, smaller, thieves' gathering. 'What a spectacle! What misery! What degradation! And yet, I question whether we, fine, easy, comfortable folks, are not greater sinners in the sight of God than are these poor wretches' (6 March 1869). Whether man became an angel or a beast largely depended, he realized, on the accidents of birth and environment; just as he also realized more clearly than some Evangelicals that it was no good telling pauperized sinners to stop sinning unless at the same time you eased the circumstances that compelled them to sin. He urged those thieves of Jackson's to go and thieve no more; but he saw their point, when they said that if they did not steal they would starve. He came away from the meeting in a state of creditable uncertainty.

From the L.C.M. and the R.S.U. and, as time went by, from the other organizations that emulated and worked along with them, there rapidly proliferated institutions to complement and complete the rescue work begun in schools and mission services. How could their children practice higher ideals of conduct if, when they left the classroom, they had nowhere to bo but Tom-All-Alone's or the iron roller in Regent's Park? Those without homes needed homes; many of those with so-called homes were better out of them. To shelter such, Refuges were established, at first just for their pupils at night, but soon as complete homes for pupils and ex-pupils as well. Such children needed to be put in the way of turning an honest penny. Industrial Schools and the *Chichester* and *Arethusa* training-ships met this need in one way, institutions like the Shoe-Blacks' Brigade and the Newsboys' Lodging House met it in another, emigration to Australia and Canada met it in a third. Particular classes of poor were found to need special study and treatment, if they were to respond to religious appeals and offers of help. Special 'moonlight' missions were aimed at prostitutes, special 'reformatories' and refuges founded to shelter them. Costermongers were discovered to live in a world and by a code of their own. A civil servant. W. J. Orsman, developed a mission to them – the Golden Lane Mission – which became a model of its kind; Shaftesbury became 'an honorary coster', and seems to have derived greater joy and satisfaction from none of his urban philanthropies during his later years; the donkey they gave him became quite famous. Orphanages were founded, to give parentless infants a better start in life than their only other resource, the poor law. For the singularly tragic class of crippled children, day-nurseries and 'cripples' parlours', hospitals and holiday-homes were started, outings and entertainments arranged. Coffee-taverns and coffee-palaces were set up to offer cheaper, healthier, less degrading refreshment and entertainment than was available in the beer-shops, gin-palaces and penny gaffs.

Such were the sort of activities which characterized what might well be called the philanthropic and religious underworld of the city. With some of them Shaftesbury was closely and continuously associated; with others more vaguely. Over all, however, his presence hovered. He was, so to speak, their patron saint. They turned out *en masse* to his memorial service in Westminster Abbey. Pall bearers came from the Bible Society, the Religious Tract Society, the Shoeblacks' Brigades, the King Edward Industrial Schools, the Y.M.C.A., the Costermongers' Mission, the Ragged Schools Union, the George Yard Ragged School, the L.C.M., the National Refuges and Training Ships. Nearly two hundred bodies in all were represented. A list of them is printed at the back of Hodder's biography. There may be seen equally the range of Shaftesbury's interests in this sphere and the distance that the philanthropic idea had travelled beyond the static parochialism of the pre-Victorian period. Present were the Pure Literature Society and the Female Preventive Institution; the St James's

Home for Female Inebriates, and the Destitute Children's Dinner Society; the Watercress and Flower Girls and the Railway Missions, the Cabmen's Shelter Fund, the Provident Surgical Appliance Society, the Missions to French in London and the Saturday Half-Holiday Movement; the Home Teaching Society for the Blind, the Discharged Prisoner's Aid Society, the Tonic Sol-fa College and dozens more from the same barrel.

There were those – an increasing number of them, as the years went by – who alleged that his undying interest in these urban philanthropies was more to the credit of his heart than his head. Socialists appreciated his concern with environment but jibbed of course at his aristocratic paternalism and fundamental pessimism. More doctrinaire individualists and voluntarists appreciated the way he sacrificed himself and urged others to sacrifice themselves in the cause of social betterment, but doubted whether he was really tough enough when dealing with the poor. They suspected he and his like were too soft and sentimental, apt to be imposed upon by scroungers and unlikely to make the proper cool calculations of social profit and loss before committing cash and service. The good men and women who came together in the later 1860s to form the Charity Organiation Society, and who had much influence in Parliament, looked at Shaftesbury this way. They itched to reduce the exuberant variety of his philanthropic empire to a simpler, bonier, more business-like system. They wondered whether it was sensible or morally justifiable to spend so much time and money on socially unpromising and economically unproductive people like cripples, lunatics and shoeblacks. They thought Shaftesbury's world was emotionally self-indulgent.

Some of these charges probably stick. To admit that, of course, is not to say more than that Shaftesbury's practice had flaws in it, like theirs. If he was inclined to be too soft, they were inclined to be too hard. He was reconciled to the odd scrounger, unwilling to scrutinize too closely the deserts of individual cases, because he understood, as they never would or could, the force of circumstance, the ogreish power of environment. One cannot deny that he was in some respects emotionally self-indulgent. The ragged school mothers' tea-meeting in Lambeth, the special service in a Hoxton music-hall, the farewell to his emigrant boys and girls at Deptford, brought the tear to his eye a little quicker, perhaps, than they need have done; the accounts he would subsequently give of such occasions might be altogether too rosy. But was it self-indulgent, emotionally or physically, in an old man to leave his fireside night after night no matter what'weather to jog across London in a cab to where his sense of duty called him? It is not clear that self-indulgence outweighed self-discipline.

Shaftesbury was of course well aware of these criticisms. He ran into them when in the late 1840s – before he learnt his lesson! – he asked Parliament to grant public money to aid his enterprises. Once, in 1848, he got £1,500 to assist ragged children's emigration. When in 1849 he tried again, he was rebuffed. He learnt the hard way that Parliament, unless driven by some sudden squall of public opinion or by some very clear proof of social self-interest, would not play a humanitarian or paternalistic part. Perhaps he took too high a tone in telling them that as an allegedly Christian legislature they ought not to 'gainsay by their actions what so many of them profess with their lips when they pray "that it may please God to defend and provide for the fatherless children and all that are desolate and oppressed "'. The way they received his plea showed that they thought it God's business, not theirs. Shaftesbury therefore, thrown back upon his own resources, unrepentantly continued to devote more and more of his time to rescuing the misfits, the outcasts, the useless, the flotsam and jetsam of the city from its dreadful clutches. He felt it was his vocation to do so. He played some part in the foundation of the Charity Organization Society, with the expressed aims of which he intelligently sympathized. But he found its guiding spirit so uncongenial that he soon withdrew from active participation; there was a tang of Cobden and Bright about it that upset him. 'I feel that my business lies in the gutter', he once said, 'and I have not the least intention to get out of it.'

He was kept in the gutter, too, by the other side of his wrestling with the city: the public health movement, in which he was prominent between 1842 and about 1855. This was certainly one of the greatest works of his life; perhaps it was, next only to his work as a Lunacy Commissioner, the greatest.[1] Of all the many lines of dealing with the condition of England question, the sanitary line was the most important. What was the point of enhancing the quality of life, while the mere possibility of life at all remained doubtful? The city was in the early nineteenth century beginning to attack life with the same savage intensity as it oppressed the poor. As its growth carried it ever further beyond the existing local authorities' powers to manage it, the city was becoming a nastier place to live in: permanently nasty and lethal for the poor, at any rate occasionally nasty and lethal for the better-off. The early public health reformers understood the causes of this horror and how to cope with it; and their greatness was, not so much that they had enough science and sense and humanity to understand this, but that they fought so bravely to bring the general public to understand it too. For the general public was only slowly converted to common sense about sanitation, and the barriers which stood in the way of reform were formidable: meanness, doctrinaire individualism, doctrinaire regard for private property rights, superstition, ignorance, quackery, stupidity, the novelty and iniquity of the idea of paying rates that would most directly benefit non-rate-payers, the odiousness of administrative practices that looked foreign, and so on – a formidable jungle of barriers, basic to most of which was simple selfishness. Nor were merely passive barriers the worst that the reformers had to deal with. They found themselves vigorously counter-attacked, accused variously of corruption, despotism, ambition, 'un-Englishness'. Every slip they made – and inevitably they did make some – was taken quick advantage of; their motives were impugned, their policies misrepresented. Their only substantial compensation for these griefs was the consciousness of lives saved, disease reduced, the city slowly

1 Incidentally, it is the side of him to which Hodder does least justice.

mastered. It was exactly the sort of campaign that Ashley
excelled in. He seems to have become interested in it about
1842: perhaps because of Chadwick's *Sanitary Report*.
He was not the first big public man to come to the aid of the
doctors and social scientists amongst whom the movement
had its diffuse origins. That distinction must be divided between Bishop Blomfield of London, whose title to be regarded
as the best of his generation rests partly on the greater interests
he showed in social questions than all but one of his mitred
brethren (Stanley of Norwich being the honourable exception);
the Shropshire landowner and M.P., Robert Slaney, a
zealous amateur of social reform; and the Marquis of
Normanby, a Yorkshire peer who had been Home Secretary
for the last two years of Melbourne's administration. Having
actually seen some of the city's worst slums – an experience
which an ordinary West Ender might easily never have, although he might pass perhaps daily by their dark narrow
entrances – these men were converted by 1839. By the end of
1844 the movement had picked up other notables. Several
voluntary societies were then formed (the standard nineteenth-
century way of setting about social progress) whose practical
measures and propaganda together brought vital momentum
to the cause. Ashley approved warmly of the Association for
Promoting Cleanliness among the Poor, and was prominent
in at least two others. With Dr Southwood Smith he founded
the Society for the Improvement of the Conditions of the
Labouring Classes, alias the Labourers' Friend Society. Its
particular concern was workers' housing, its method the
financing of model dwellings by offering philanthropic capital
a return of four per cent. (Seven per cent was about the
minimum then thought commercially worthwhile.) Many
distinguished people including the Prince Consort were
persuaded to patronize this society; and undoubtedly it did
much good, not so much by the quantity of dwellings it
constructed as by setting an example which became quite
widely followed, most notably by Sir Sidney Waterlow's
Improved Industrial Dwellings Company and George
Peabody's Trust, twenty years or so later.

Of more immediate importance was the Health of Towns Association. Its avowed object was propagandist – to

diffuse among the people the information obtained by recent inquiries, as to the physical and moral evils that result from the present defective sewerage, drainage, supply of water, air and light, and construction of dwelling houses: and also for the purpose of assisting the legislature to carry into practical operation any effectual and general measures of relief, by preparing the public mind for the change.

To help with this preparation, good men of every sort of politics and men of no politics at all formed a common platform: Ashley and his evangelical high Tory friend Sir Robert Inglis, young Mr Disraeli and his well-meaning friend Lord John Manners; the rather High-Church Bishop Blomfield and the decidedly Broad-Church Bishop Stanley; Lords Normanby and Morpeth, representing the great Whig cousinhood; civil engineers like Henry Austin (who soon interested his brother-in-law Charles Dickens in it); medicos like Southwood Smith and John Simon; metropolitan councillors and parliamentary radicals, with Edwin Chadwick as a power-house behind the scenes. They made speeches, wrote articles and pamphlets, and founded provincial and suburban branches to whip up public pressure and to publicize as widely as they could the official and professional reports and writings which were beginning to flood out. They conducted several sanitary surveys of their own; the most important was of the metropolis itself. They got up petitions to support legislation, and made sure that fatuous or vicious criticism (such as came especially from threatened interests in the City of London) got answered. They made many enemies.

Ashley took his share in this congenial work; but it was not until 1848 that he became pre-eminent. That he did so then was the doing of the friend of his youth, the amiable, pious and conscientious Lord Morpeth, heir to the earldom of Carlisle and all the magnificence of Castle Howard, a member of Lord John Russell's cabinet as First Commissioner of Woods and Forests. This post made him *ex officio* president of the General Board of Health, the long overdue central authority set up by the Public Health Act which he had himself fought through the Commons, unsuccessfully in 1847, successfully in 1848. This new Board, equipped with large emergency powers to handle the current cholera epidemic, and less large but still striking powers to cover urban Britain with local sanitary authorities, was to have two members besides himself. He chose, after-events were to suggest, not wisely but too well; he chose the two strongest men he could – Edwin Chadwick and Lord Ashley, with Southwood Smith as a fourth, medical commissioner for so long as the cholera lasted.

These four men, to whom the future happiness of millions of their fellow-creatures was thus confided, formed an interesting company. They got on extremely well together. This could not confidently have been predicted. Ashley's diary shows that he had since 1833 at least been rather jealous of Morpeth, very quick to censure him on many questions. Southwood Smith was a Unitarian, which to Ashley was equivalent to nothing at all. Chadwick, who seems to have been an unmilitant agnostic, was married to the daughter of one of Manchester's biggest millowners, and earlier in his career had primed Althorp and other Whig ministers with arguments against the Ten-Hours' Bill. The members of the General Board of Health had little in common beyond their zeal for sanitary reform. That, however, was so strong that it made them fast friends, harmonious and untiring colleagues. It was a common religion for them. The sanitary blue books were their scriptures; cholera, typhus, smallpox, diphtheria, dysentery and premature death stood for the devil; the vision of a city from which had been eliminated all avoidable environmental causes of pain and poverty was their nearest approach to heaven on earth. Whatever Smith's and Chadwick's formal faith, they felt these things at least as passionately as Morpeth and Ashley, who expressed themselves in orthodox Christian terms.

Court of Sewers at 10, after which . . . went to the worst places going in Southwark, Bermondsey etc. We saw dreadful abominations. . . . I hope we are gradually doing some good. God of love and pity! grant that we may; smooth our path, make the way, let ours be a voice of health and message of comfort to these festering haunts and squalid hordes! [recorded Morpeth on 23 November 1848.]

Morpeth was a good Christian; yet Morpeth was not after all so concerned with the sanitary idea as the others. He was not permanently haunted by it as they were. He could – indeed he did, after a couple of years of excellent work – give it up and retire. The others could never quite forget it. Smith and Chadwick pursued it remorselessly to the ends of their lives; and although Ashley had other things to think about, the fears and miseries of the city were always there at the back of his mind, a *faux-bourdon* of horror. It even spoilt his holidays. His doctor once told him to go to Ems to take the waters there and at all costs to *stop worrying*. But the doctor was asking too much. The heat of summer only made it worse:

I cannot obey the doctor – as I lie panting under the influence of the sun, surrounded by clean air and fresh smells, I reflect with pain and shame and grief on the condition of others who, under a sun equally powerful, are tortured by foul gas, exhalations – human, vegetable, putrescent – without, perhaps, a drink of wholesome water to assuage their thirst. [15 July 1852.]

It is no disparagement of Morpeth, to whom the hard and critical Chadwick was attached as he was to no other minister he ever met, to doubt whether his retirement at Castle Howard was spoilt the same way.

The General Board of Health did great things during the five years that were allowed it. It did so much, indeed, and attempted so much more, in such a manner, that it dug its own grave. Vested interests of many kinds lobbied and scribbled against it. After Morpeth went in 1850, there followed a procession of lesser men, who neither knew nor cared much about it: first the insouciant, rude Lord Seymour, then the dim and spineless Lord John Manners, finally the conceited Sir William Molesworth. Ashley's elevation to the peerage in 1851 removed the Board's best spokesman in the Commons; Ebrington and other enthusiasts did their best, but they had little of Ashley's power. Public opinion was still insufficiently educated in sanitation to be able to detect and resist arguments essentially irrelevant, ignorant, or base. Moreover, some of the arguments deployed against the Board were reasonable ones; and not all the men who deployed them were base. It was Chadwick's misfortune to be so often right that he simply could not conceive being wrong. In fact, he was, now and then, wrong. He was not the only expert. On one or two matters the bulk of expert opinion ran against him; on a few more, experts might quite legitimately differ; and Chadwick was such a dogmatic dynamo of a man that even when he was right and everybody knew he was right, his way of doing things was apt to put people's backs up. Morpeth and Ashley did not mind him, because they appreciated Chadwick's essential worth; and they gallantly conceived it a duty and a privilege, while associated with him, to 'stage-manage' Chadwick so far as he would let them. 'I continue to think Chadwick has greater powers of doing good than anyone else,' wrote Morpeth in his diary when he retired from the fray; 'but his yoke-fellow's is an uneasy place.'[1] 'Our friend is very wrong-headed, and must be controlled,' Ashley once told Morpeth; and, on another occasion: 'Chadwick showed me your note; I am glad you wrote it – our friend's infirmity is that of being a little disposed to use authority instead of persuasion. . . .'[2] They tried to save Chadwick from himself, and to some extent succeeded; but too much of his fiery genius slipped past their guard, and tragically helped to bring about the Board's collapse.

Nevertheless, while the General Board of Health survived, it accomplished great things It laid the foundations of British public health; it established a network of local health authorities for subsequent legislators and administrators (chief among them, Dr John Simon, who took over Chadwick's role as mainspring of sanitary reform) to improve and extend; it showed how the dreadful new scourge of epidemic cholera (new, that is, to Britain) could be combated; it began that

1. 27 March 1850.
2. Letters of 18 and 21 January 1850. Castle Howard Letter-Books, 2nd series, book 59.

accumulation of expert knowledge, that process of continuous research and inquiry, which was and always must be pre-requisite to any effective system of social welfare.

This was a great work; and Ashley's share in it seems to fall into three compartments. First, he was assiduous in attendance to its administrative business; he slaved like the rest of them during the crises of the cholera epidemic; he became as expert in sanitary matters as he did in those of lunacy.[1] Second, he used all his personal authority, influence and force to protect the Board against its enemies within the adminis-tration itself. These struggles were not apparent to the world at large, but recent research has shown how fierce they were, and how nearly the Board's enemies in the Treasury – then, as ever, narrow and shortsighted in its attitude to expenditure on great social objects – and the cabinet succeeded in squash-ing it.[2] While Morpeth was still in the Government, they had a friend at court; but after he went, no friend worth the name until Palmerston's arrival at the Home Office in 1853; and it seems reasonable to suppose that he only showed the sym-pathy he did because of the love he bore Ashley. The hated Chadwick and the mild Southwood Smith would have been helpless without Ashley to take up the cudgels for them; as he did with all the greater zest, for disliking Seymour almost as much, in a different way, as he disliked John Bright.

Ashley's third contribution to the work of the Board was the management of its work in Parliament. Before he went to the Lords in June 1851 this meant the introduction of a series of important and often complicated measures. Two of them demand special notice, as having been so closely connected with everything he most cared about that they have been generally known as Ashley's (or Shaftesbury's; he had the singular fortune to see them safely through both Houses!)

1 He was not so assiduous as Chadwick and Smith; but then, he was not paid for the work, and he had plenty of other business to manage besides. Attendance figures are given in *Parliamentary Papers*, 1854 (1768), xxxv. 54.

2 See the admirable books of S. E. Finer, *The Life and Times of Sir Edwin Chadwick*, and R. A. Lewis, *Edwin Chadwick and the Public Health Movement*.

Lodging Houses Acts. No doubt they were 'got up' for him by
Chadwick or some other professional;[1] but they were peculiarly
his own, inasmuch as lodging-houses had been troubling him
for nearly ten years. The term lodging-houses, with its sugges-
tions of furnished rooms for single gentlemen, is unlikely to
send thrills of horror down modern spines. Ashley's interest
in lodging-houses is therefore all too likely to be misunder-
stood. They were in fact among the most horrible places where
poor people had to live. Where did new arrivals in the city
put up while seeking, as at first they optimistically might,
agreeable accommodation? A lodging-house, almost certainly.
And where did they live when no agreeable accommodation
occurred? A lodging-house, quite often. Lodging-houses met
a pressing need in the early Victorian city, and so were
numerous. They had roofs, and offered food and company
of a kind. Some – the more expensive – might be relatively
clean and respectable; Sam Weller's 'twopenny rope' was
probably one such; but most were cheap and very, very nasty.
The early sanitarians quickly singled them out as primary
public enemies; diseases, nourished in their airless crowded
rooms, spread easily wherever their inmates went in search
of charity or occupation. Ashley had every reason for loathing
such 'sinks of wretchedness and vice', such homes and
nurseries of crime, promiscuity and prostitution. In an article
he contributed to the *Quarterly Review* in 1847 he described
two such houses he knew of. In one of seven rooms were
'stowed, besides children, sixty adults, a goodly company
of males and females of every profession of fraud and violence,
with a very few poor and industrious labourers. . . .' In the
other's main room, fifteen feet by ten feet, twenty-seven adults,
thirty-one children, and several dogs; upstairs in a room
twelve feet by ten feet, thirty-two persons in six beds; up yet
again, 'up an ascent more like a flue than a staircase', to four
tiny rooms, all crammed – the whole a scene of 'dirt, confusion

1 See Lewis, *op. cit.*, p. 346. It would be a mistake to read too much
into this. Chadwick was on his death-bed when he used the phrase;
and Hodder's book had – understandably enough – made him very
angry. But Ashley could not possibly have drawn them up himself.

and obscenity'. Describing another in his big speech on emigration in 1848, Ashley quoted a city missionary as saying it was so dirty that the bugs fell rattling on his hat like peas.

The Acts he promoted in 1851 were well calculated to improve this state of affairs. One broke new ground by placing common lodging-houses under the control of local authorities, requiring such houses to be licensed and to be open to inspection both by police and medical officers of health. The other was a permissive Act, empowering large local authorities to build their own model lodging-houses and pay for them out of the rates. This introduction of the principle of 'council housing' broke new ground too, and might have been the means of much social benefit, had more than three authorities – and they but timorously – taken it up. Ashley's mind, as so often when social welfare was concerned, was running way ahead of his generation. Only the Regulation and Inspection Act therefore came to anything; and very successful it was. Medical authorities reported a striking improvement in the healthiness of such houses, the police reported on a diminution of their criminality. Charles Dickens, whose knowledge of the city was not less expert than Shaftesbury's, told him that it was 'the best law . . . ever passed by an English parliament'; and, considering that Dickens never concealed his dislike of some of Shaftesbury's works – he once described him as 'a kind of amiable bull in a china-shop of good intentions'[1] – that testimony is not to be taken lightly.

1 Letter to Miss Burdett-Coutts, 12 August 1850. He also wrote in *The Examiner*, 19 August 1848, that 'It might be laid down as a very good rule of social and political guidance, that whatever Exeter Hall champions, is the thing by no means to be done.' Shaftesbury tried hard to be just to Dickens, but never really succeeded in forgiving him his scepticism about ragged schools.

EPILOGUE

NOT the least remarkable thing about Lord Shaftesbury is that, even in his own day, his virtues were allowed far to outweigh his vices. For he was in some ways, in some moods, an awkward and disagreeable man: proud, impetuous, self-righteous, vain, violent, suspicious, censorious. Most of these worse qualities of his were obvious enough to his contemporaries. Not, indeed, quite all of them. Fierce though his feelings often were, he was usually capable of concealing them when it would have been unprofitable or, by his code of aristocratic conduct, eccentric to show them. But what he could not say or show in public he would hastily and angrily set down in his diary; and many who had supposed they knew him well must have been as surprised and pained as Gladstone was when he read certain selected extracts from that copious diary in Edwin Hodder's official biography, five years after Shaftesbury's death. 'I coud not have believed', he wrote, 'from the constantly kind relations between us that I could have presented to one sustaining those relations a picture of such unredeemed and universal blackness. . . . I am now inclined to regret what I had used to reflect upon with pleasure, that I had broken bread at Lord Shaftesbury's table, for he must have been a reluctant host.'[1] His regrets would have been the keener had he read some of the parts of the diary that Hodder did not print.

Yet however necessary it may be to insist that Shaftesbury was not the simple, genial, pious, soft-hearted philanthropist of popular legend and much popular writing, no truths will ever be discovered about him that can conceivably lessen his stature as one of the greatest Victorians, and, in however curious a manner, one of the best. Nor, obviously, is he one of those men, allegedly great, whose greatness passed unrecognized in his own day. When he had only been in public life for fifteen years or so, he was already being acclaimed as an especially admirable man; and men of better-established

1 British Museum, Additional Manuscripts, 44773, fos. 13–33.

positions than his, in politics and society alike, were going further to meet his often troublesome demands, and to forgive his sometimes cantankerous conduct, than they would bother to do in respect of anyone else, precisely because they perceived in him unusual strength and goodness. His strength and goodness were not unusual because such qualities were in themselves uncommon in those years. There was, if one may so speak of it, an enormous quantity of goodness circulating in society, a widely diffused urge to better the human lot and elevate the human mind, exacting from those who felt it a contribution of service and money which was probably greater (in proportion to the means of those who gave it) than ever before or since; and more was not achieved by all this charitable effort, only because the conditions it was trying to remedy were so intractable. In self-sacrifice and generosity, Shaftesbury was indeed eminent among his contemporaries. But he was something more besides. He was in many ways representative; he was also, in some ways, unique.

Lord Shaftesbury's especial claim to greatness was that he personified the conscience of his age, the early Victorian age. Born in 1801, he made no mark in public life until the early thirties. His best years lay between the later twenties and the sixties. Thereafter he became increasingly a survival, and an anachronism. It was in the early Victorian years, during most of which he was plain Lord Ashley, that his best work was done, that the lever of his moral and physical energies was applied most scientifically, that his true uniqueness showed. This was the product of several factors. He was an aristocrat. He was clever. He could easily have made a successful political career, holding ministerial office when the Tories were in and lucrative administrative or decorative posts when they were not. Such a career had its attractions for a man whose birth suggested it, whose natural talents would have made it easy and prosperous, and who was, for the son of an English earl, relatively poor. His father and mother thought him a fool for not taking it up. His uniqueness lay largely in his having deliberately rejected it. That rejection was made on conscientious grounds. He conceived himself committed to a cause – at first, that of the factory workers, and later, that of the most helpless and destitute classes of society – which forbade attachment to any one party. The members of the cabinets to which he would otherwise have belonged thought his decision quixotic, but admirable. They respected it as an uncommon act of conscience; and, soon thereafter, everyone in the political world was respecting him on similar grounds.

No eminent lay Victorian was more obviously and unremittingly guided by conscience. Most Victorians, of course, were more or less guided by conscience. Theirs was an uncommonly conscientious age. They took it for granted that the claims of duty and pleasure were, up to a point which each individual must fix for himself, irreconcilable. They accepted the fact that conscience might make life uncomfortable. And so they accepted Lord Shaftesbury, although he sometimes made life as uncomfortable for others as he made it for himself. His acceptance and high standing in the close-knit political world of his hey-day reflected the reasons for his national celebrity in shorter, clearer focus. Men admired him and put up with him when he behaved extravagantly because they saw consuming him a principle which few of them would have dared to carry to the same lengths. This did not mean that they always thought him right. Sometimes it was simply that their consciences directed a different course from his. Shaftesbury never understood either of the two main grounds on which such a different course might conscientiously be urged. These grounds might be religious, or political. When they were the former, the result merely of a different view of the case deriving, as it usually did in that age of faith, from a different idea of the Christian religion, Shaftesbury's failure to understand and quickness to condemn were often lamentable – though it must be admitted that he was no worse in this respect than many of his contemporaries. But sometimes the sources of such a thwarting of Shaftesbury's will, and the grounds on which conscientious statesmen would justify it, were of a more 'political' kind; and here it is not so certain that Shaftesbury was wrong. At any rate, the questions which he was the first great modern parliamentarian clearly to pose are still matter of urgent discussion. Is political morality a different thing from personal? Must a man leave his private conscience behind him when he goes into politics? – and if so, how can he tell when (if ever) he ought to take it up again? How far should respect for the established order be allowed to hold up or to modify radical reforms, upon the *abstract* desirability of which all men might agree? Is it better to participate in an admittedly imperfect form of government and society, attempting to improve them from within, or to keep clear of them and press improvements from without? Upon the whole, Shaftesbury chose the latter part. One cannot be sure that he was thereby showing a livelier conscience than the politicians who accepted the existing order as a necessary vehicle for government without necessarily failing to see in how many respects it needed to be changed. Some of those, certainly, whom Shaftesbury denounced as heartless, had no less heart than he; they differed in having stronger stomachs. Yet without the Shaftesburys of their age (and he was only the most conspicuous and forceful of his kind) their hearts might have become, by insensible degrees, insensitive, their efforts towards reform relaxed; and the better of them knew it. The high respect in which they held Shaftesbury rested, at bottom, on their recognizing that their differences of opinion from him – so painful when they occurred – were an inevitable price to be paid for the advantages of living in a free and Christian society, a burden to be manfully borne; that his relentless, gallant and fruitful endeavours for the public weal set an example of social responsibility and personal sacrifice at a level where it was as valuable as it was uncommon; and that, although a society with too many Shaftesburys would be a fearful experience, one without any would be far worse.

COSTERMONGER'S BARROW PURCHASED BY LORD
SHAFTESBURY WHEN HE WAS ENROLLED
AS A COSTERMONGER, 1875

POSTSCRIPT

Nothing has been published during the past ten years to diminish the possible usefulness of this book, as an up-to-date view of Shaftesbury the man as well as of his work, fixed firmly in his very Victorian times. Such a book did not exist when I wrote this one; nor does it yet exist. Meanwhile, the reissue of this study gives me a welcome opportunity to enlarge its chances of usefulness by saying something more than I originally said about the earlier books on Shaftesbury, and by calling readers' attention to the most valuable recent writings on him.

The great standard biography of Shaftesbury was and is that of his Victorian Admirer Edwin Hodder (1886); I paid my respects to it in my Preface. The rest of the Shaftesbury literature, which was plentiful enough, seemed to me pretty worthless, whether published after the Great War or before it. Almost all of the many books and booklets written about him this side of 1918 were either shallow-rooted exercises in popularisation or historically care-free hagiographies. I thought it a waste of time and space to notice them at all, and thus slipped into the ungracious mistake of neglecting to mention specifically the one book of that epoch which was distinctively different and in a class of its own: *Lord Shaftesbury*, by J. L. and Barbara Hammond first published in 1923.

I am glad to have this opportunity to clarify my opinions about the Hammonds' book. Its coverage of Shaftesbury's public works was admirable. Many of them (all but his expressly religious works and the religious elements of his other works) were just the sort of thing the Hammonds most cared for and knew a lot about, and they did them ample justice. They knew so much, indeed, that it hardly mattered that they were writing without benefit of the post-1945 wave of Victorian studies upon which my more severe exercises in selection and digestion could rest. As for the Hammonds' understanding of the times Shaftesbury lived in, that too was in general remarkably alert and well-informed, enabling them to support their subject with suitably detailed backcloths at all appropriate moments. But their perspectives and proportions were not, I thought, faultless. They chose to write relatively little about the man himself, and, what was more likely to reduce the historical value of their book, they did not like, and made no bones about not liking, what mattered more to Shaftesbury than anything else: his kind of religion. With the content, context, and foundations of his Evangelicalism they had nothing like the extensive familiarity they had with the other sides of his life; and it was this lack which chiefly accounted for their failure, as it seemed to me, to provide a credible and properly rounded portrait of the man. Perhaps they simply did not 'like' him enough to do that. Whatever the reason, the book they had written, with all its strong virtues, seemed so different from the book I had written that the two had little to do with each other, and crossed each others' paths not at all. I regret that my failure to say this ten years ago could have encouraged the supposition that I set a lower value on their book than was in fact the case.

Those ten years have been busy ones for Victorian scholarship. The advantages which I enjoyed in surveying Shaftesbury's century forty years after the Hammonds are probably less great than the advantages enjoyed by the historian doing the same thing ten years after me, so fast now flows the flood of research and publication; which is one of the reasons why Geoffrey Finlayson of the University of Glasgow (who has at his disposal more than twice the quantity of words than were at mine, and who has kept abreast of this flood better than I) should, in about two years, be able to give us at last the solid professional historian's biography Shaftesbury so richly deserves, and set him safely on rocks of scholarship untouched by the waves of religious enthusiasm and soft-hearted – not to say soft-headed – sentimentality which may confidently be expected to continue to launch books about him. Readers who want a foretaste of Mr Finlayson's book will find it in his essay on Shaftesbury (as, in particular, an organiser and leader of public opinion) in a book being published just as I write these words: *Pressure from Without*, edited by Patricia Hollis (1974).

I am happy in conclusion to call attention to those publications of the last ten years which are most likely to satisfy readers' desires for more detailed (and, in respect especially of housing, more up-to-date) handlings of matters I had to pass over rather quickly. About working-class housing in particular there are excellent recent writings. Two of them are by John Tarn: *Working-Class Housing in 19th Century Britain* (1971) and *Five Per Cent Philanthropy: an Account of Housing in Urban Areas between 1840 and 1914* (1973). Enid Bauldie is helpful in *Cruel Habitations. A History of Working Class Housing, 1780–1918* (1974). Then there are several excellent essays, finely illustrated, in parts III and VI of H. J. Dyos and M. Wolff, *The Victorian City: Images and Realities* (2 v. 1973); this great work indeed includes scholarly material on almost every aspect of Victorian city life with which Shaftesbury concerned himself, and must be a primary port of call for all future inquirers. Lunacy, about the treatment of which Shaftesbury cared so much, has not yet attracted anything like as much interest as housing, but W. L. Parry-Jones has carried some parts of the story further than I did in *The Trade in Lunacy: A Study of Private Madhouses in England in the 18th and 19th Centuries* (1972). Some formidable research into the factory movement is being conducted by John Foster of Strathclyde University. Whether Shaftesbury's place in that movement will be much altered by it, we shall have to wait and see. Meanwhile there is an admirable chapter by J. T. Ward summarising the story as it at present stands in his book *Popular Movements c. 1830–1850* (1970). As for the religious world in which Shaftesbury lived and moved and had his being, a gap which I am equally astonished and ashamed to have left is filled by Clyde Binfield, *George Williams and the Y.M.C.A.; a Study in Victorian Social Attitudes* (1973).

GEOFFREY BEST 1974

NOTE ON THE ILLUSTRATION OF EXETER HALL

Exeter Hall stood on the north side of the Strand, just to the west of where Aldwych leaves it, and adjacent to the old Lyceum Theatre. Designed by Gandy Deering and completed in 1831, it became at once the centre of the Evangelical and the metropolitan musical worlds. Many religious societies had their central offices in the building, which acquired so strongly Evangelical a savour that all who were anxious not to be taken for Evangelicals, or associated with them, kept well away from it. The largest of its three halls, twice extended, could hold three thousand people at the anniversary meetings of religious societies, special meetings or services, or musical concerts for which it was renowned. The most notable of the last-named were the massive oratorio performances of the Sacred Harmonic Society; the biggest in Britain, until the Crystal Palace became available. One of the peculiar excellences of its orchestra, said John Timbs (*Curiosities of London*, 1868, p. 334), was that 'every member could see the conductor.'

INDEX